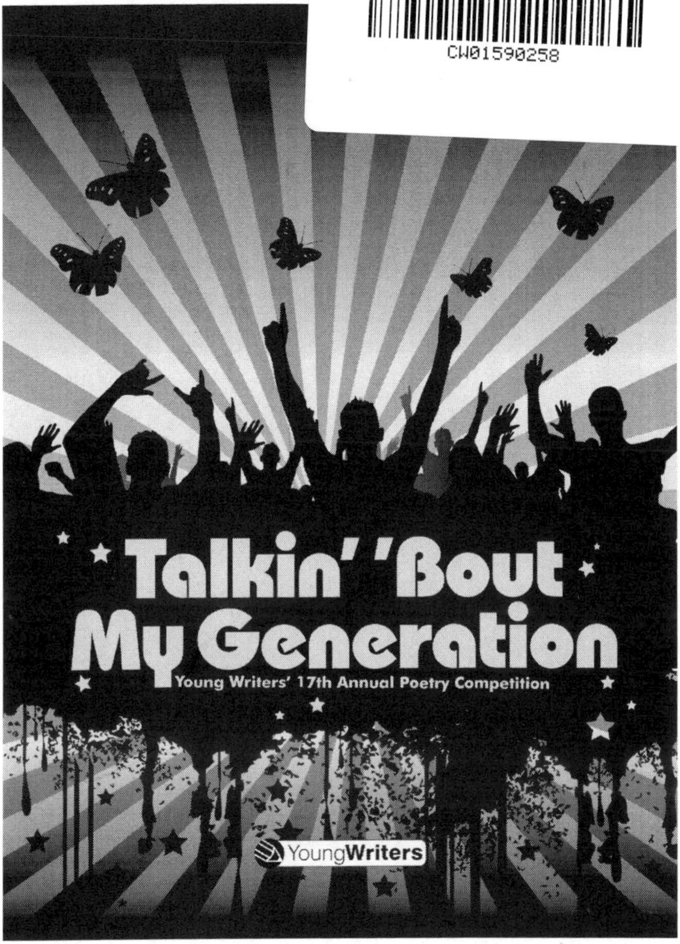

Poems From Lancashire

Edited by Donna Samworth

YoungWriters
First published in Great Britain in 2008 by:
Young Writers
Remus House
Coltsfoot Drive
Peterborough
PE2 9JX
Telephone: 01733 890066
Website: www.youngwriters.co.uk

SB ISBN 978-1 84431 436 2

Foreword

This year, the Young Writers' *Talkin' 'Bout My Generation* competition proudly presents a showcase of the best poetic talent selected from thousands of up-and-coming writers nationwide.

Young Writers was established in 1991 to promote the reading and writing of poetry within schools and to the young of today. Our books nurture and inspire confidence in the ability of young writers and provide a snapshot of poems written in schools and at home by budding poets of the future.

The thought, effort, imagination and hard work put into each poem impressed us all and the task of selecting poems was a difficult but nevertheless enjoyable experience.

We hope you are as pleased as we are with the final selection and that you and your family continue to be entertained with *Talkin' 'Bout My Generation Poems From Lancashire* for many years to come.

Contents

The Poems

Dreamed Up!

In my dream
I work with the RSPCA
Helping animals every day.

In my dream
I can help horses, dogs, cats, birds,
Rabbits, hens and chickens.

In my dream
I like to do show-jumping in competitions.

In my dream
I would like to go in dressage with my horse.

Out of dreams
Woke up!

Abigail Allen (11)
Broadfield Specialist School

Dreamed Up

In my dream
I am a vet who cares for animals who are in danger.

In my dream
I help cure pets for examples cats, dogs, rabbits.

In my dream
I even help abandoned animals.

In my dream
I treat the abandoned animals
And give them to the RSPCA.

Out of dreams,
Woke up!

Simone Stratton (11)
Broadfield Specialist School

Dreamed Up!

In my dream
I am a Hollywood star.

In my dream
I drive a fancy car.

In my dream
I have lots of money.

In my dream
I am very funny.

Out of dreams,
Woke up!

Alex Tarrega (11)
Broadfield Specialist School

Dreamed Up

In my dream
I am very strong

In my dream
I lift heavy weights

In my dream
I have lots of money

In my dream
I win trophies.

Out of dreams,
Woke up!

Bradley Youd (11)
Broadfield Specialist School

Dreamed Up

In my dream
I went to the vets then I had a debt.

In my dream
I was a vet to pay the debt.

In my dream
I was a vet
Then I had a big bet.

In my dream
I went to bed
Then I saw a jet.

Out of dreams,
Woke up!

John Kyme (11)
Broadfield Specialist School

Dreamed Up!

In my dream
I am a Hot Wheels driver.

In my dream
I win all the races.

In my dream
I win lots of trophies.

In my dream
I am a champion.

Out of dream,
Woke up!

Ben Littlewood (11)
Broadfield Specialist School

A Tribute To Rhys Jones

A killer walks the street at night
After taking the life of one so bright.
Rhys did not deserve to die so young,
11 years old he'd done no wrong
So young Rhys was taken up above God
Took him in his hands of love
To play the game he loved so much
This shocking death just broke the hearts of everyone he loved.

Yesterday was just a memory
Our laughter was sunny and bright
Then the clouds started to gather
When we heard you were out of sight.
So now Rhys Jones plays so happily
To the angels in the crowd and
Every time he hits the net
They roar his name out loud
As his parents repeated appeals
Saying that someone could help
To find the killer
That took the life of one so bright.

So peace to you little Blue boy Rhys
Till your family join you up there
Not a halo out of place, the little ace soccer star
Has no fear to face.
For football he loved and played, Everton home and away
He wore the blue shirt proudly and spoke the name with pride
God put him in His best eleven and there he plays up in Heaven.

By his family and friends he's missed so much
Because now he's not here to touch
Forever he will be protected from harm as he stays by God's
right arm.

The hooded killer is still here,
But he still has God's wrath to fear.

Emma Bunting (12)
Burscough Priory Science College

Midsummer Monsoon

Take cover
Mother Nature is attacking
Torrential rain and thunderstorms strike without stopping
6ft up and everything buried
Apart from in cities which keep on growing.

In just 2 hours a month's rainfall drowns Britain
999 calls are hitten
Lightning strikes and houses light
The houses are dying, dying, dying.

Only ducks and small children are enjoying the rain
Whilst others are trying to help ease the strain
Of all the rain.

Chaos abounds on the roads and tracks
People hurry about with umbrellas and macs
6 week holidays have just begun
But it doesn't look like there will be much fun.

Jonathan Gibbons (12)
Burscough Priory Science College

McCann Innocence Poem

Sadness, disgrace and aggression
This is that the McCanns feel.
Why would someone accuse the McCanns?
Of killing the little baby Madeleine
How can the police say this ludicrous thing?
To kill your own child your love
A part of you, her little baby Madeleine
They will always stand strong
Together, helping supporting each other
Over these very terrible times
Poor baby Madeleine
Why would someone do such a thing?
Take someone's baby away from them
Their little baby Madeleine.

James Harrison (12)
Burscough Priory Science College

September 11th

September 11th, day of debris,
Day the Towers ceased to be,
Day they crumbled down to the dead,
Day of the death of the people they lead.

September 11th, day of the sad,
Day their relatives became so mad,
Day they wept for their sibling's soul,
Day their loved ones became no more.

September 11th, day of the lucky,
Day they washed their child whom was mucky,
Because the delay their lives were spared,
Because someone up there obviously cared.

September 11th, remember that date,
And take a minute to think of their fate,
Think of those, whose friends had died,
And think of those terrorists whose religion had lied.

Anna Gore (12)
Burscough Priory Science College

The Falling Towers

The planes curtain railed the Twin Towers but the Islamic extremists didn't bail
As the Washington maul was mauled that happened in dire need.

The fires spread like chocolate spread
The planes smashing into the Towers like a football in a goal,
For the terrorists had accomplished their goal.

Tragedy hit our Majesty within the hour,
For the firefighters were rescuing the people,
For some people it was the last day they would ever see.

For the deals were done and could not be undone,
For the people that died we are sorry
And your lives will not be forgotten.

Connor Slowey (12)
Burscough Priory Science College

The Big Match

At the beginning of the game
Someone was kicked and went lame
Everton were winning the game
Until Liverpool were drawing the same.

Liverpool fans were chanting and Liverpool were going to score
Until Everton came behind them and Yobo scored once more
It's the end of the first half and there was a sea of blue scarves.

Now they start from scratch
On the second part of the match
The second half is tough
Because all the players are rough
The time is running slow
But you still have to watch the time you know.

This may be the final score
Because it looks like it's going to end in a draw
It's nearly the end
But you will never guess what
Everton score once more
So all the fans cheered on the spot.

James Clarke (12)
Burscough Priory Science College

Missing Girl

Guilty, guilty, are they guilty?
Trying to clear their name
Lie detector tests to boost their campaign.
Disappeared body as sad as it may seem
People pointing their fingers make the McCanns scream.
Looking for their little girl, sends their heads into a whirl,
Oh where can she bo? If only we could see.
Keep her safe, keep her fine,
She is never out of our minds.

Luke Miszczak (12)
Burscough Priory Science College

Gold Miners

Find the thousands, find the thousands, find the thousands
Half a mile underground
Keep on going down and down
Nowhere to be found
Lost 3000.

Deep down in the Johannesburg mine
Worried that they have been trapped for some time
In the dark they cower
What has happened to the power?
Sad 3000.

Cramped conditions searing heat
To escape is no mean feat
Six hours starting to suffocate underground
The emergency exit must be found
Hopeful 3000.

Find the thousands, find the thousands, find the thousands
Into the darkness a chink of light
The workers thought it was a beautiful sight
The sound of voices up above
Back to the ones they love
Thankful 3000.

Thomas Ashcroft (12)
Burscough Priory Science College

Four Held After Gunfight Killing

'Voice on radio'
Magda Pnewski, a Polish woman,
Caught in a crossfire, last Thursday night,
Three men and a woman, arrested,
A VW car, recovered,
No weapon found . . .

She arrived from Poland, four years ago,
And has worked as an activities co-ordinator,
At the BUPA run
She had boyfriend, a sister, a friend,
And witnesses after her deadly end.

The Det Ch Insp said that she was an innocent woman,
And that the weapons used, should now be banned,
Drug dealers and illegal events taken place,
Scientists are now on the case.

The sound of the gun as she hit the ground.
No witnesses could make a sound.
Family and friends began to cry,
From the moment when she started to die,
They wiped the tears from their face,
As goes on the human race.

Amal Abufares (12)
Burscough Priory Science College

Burscough Blasters Get The Game

Burscough Blasters get the game,
The town of Hucknall leave to shame.
Out of the stadium, out of the town,
Leaving the place with their heads so down.

The game begins with bad defence,
To them the field seemed very dense.
'Pass to the player! Charge for the goal!'
Zooming towards like a speedy shoal.

Tired but happy, into the goal,
Leaping up from the deep dark hole.
All of the players are running away,
The lead they have is going to stay!

Hucknall level in the 28th minute,
They're now sure they're going to win it.
Burscough and the ball are running away,
The lead they have is going to stay!

A long time later in the 78th minute,
A booth blast makes sure they're going to win it.
There it is, the final goal,
The crowd are roaring like a lion in a hole.

Burscough blasters get the game,
The town of Hucknall leave in shame.
Out of the stadium, out of the town,
Leaving the place with their heads so down!

Graham Boreham (12)
Burscough Priory Science College

Teeth

Our teeth are important
In everyday life
A check-up is needed the dentist will check
For disease and abcesses,
Plaque and infection.

He will tell you how,
To look after your teeth
We should use a toothbrush
Three times a day
Put on the toothpaste
And brush away.

Brush up and down
And all around
Clean for two minutes
Then floss and rinse
Wipe your mouth
Then put your toothbrush away.

If you eat too many sweet things
You can get infected gums
Teeth can come loose
And even fall out
Do as you are told
And your teeth will stay shiny and white.

Laura Mercer (12)
Burscough Priory Science College

My World

Dear Lord

I can't believe she's gone,
I can't believe she's gone,
Wherever she is please look down on her,
And make sure she's safe.

Little Madeleine,
You are my world,
You're sun, moon, star and sea,
You are my little angel,
So wherever you are please come home.

We all miss you dearly,
Our hearts are broken in two,
I hope you can hear me,
You are our world that is slowly breaking in two.

Amen.

Emma Potter (13)
Burscough Priory Science College

The 11th Of September 2001

The 11th of September 2001
So much destruction, so many things gone.

Fires are blazing, smoke rising high
So many people were going to die.

Debris falling off the Towers so tall
Some of the people had no choice but to fall.

The Twin Towers of New York City
Now they are gone, it's such a pity.

Six years on we haven't forgotten about the terror that day
That was such a shock.

The 11th of September 2001
So much destruction, so many things gone.

Rowan Sanderson (12)
Burscough Priory Science College

A Gun Shot To The Boy

Innocent boy walking home,
After footy practice near the pub,
Having a kick about with his mates,
When a boy rides up on his bike.

Pulls out a gun and aims at the man,
Rhys' friends ducked down behind the van,
The man shoots, hits the car, all its windows,
Shattering down.

Hitting Rhys in the back of the neck,
He falls to the ground
Blood spreading all around,
All that was left of him, nothing.

Sirens from ambulances all around,
Mother's crying on the ground,
As she rests Rhys on her arm,
Rhys is now gone forever.

Rebecca Pickering (13)
Burscough Priory Science College

Southport Air Show, The Famous Red Arrows

Sat on Southport seafront,
Spectators were amazed.
For the Red Arrows shooting past,
Which made them all gaze.
Blue, red and white clouds,
Lines across the sky,
They disappear as time goes by.
Many people came to watch,
But sadly the show stopped.
Until Sunday,
Tomorrow.

Megan Walker (12)
Burscough Priory Science College

The Nutcracker

The smell of fresh cooking on Christmas Eve,
Grandfather Drosselmeyer arrives.
He gives Clara a beautiful Nutcracker,
And Fritz soldiers with toy knives.
Fritz is jealous of her joy,
And with that he breaks the toy.
Clara's upset about what has become
Of her beautiful Nutcracker.

As the clock strikes midnight,
She shrinks to the size of a mouse.
Everything is bigger, everything is larger,
In her beautiful house.
The room fills with an army of mice,
Not a single one is very nice.
They fight and they battle, but are not good enough
To beat the almighty Nutcracker.

The Nutcracker takes Clara to a land of snow,
A place where nobody else will go
This new world, an enchanted land.
As they walk through hand in hand,
Silent snowflakes fall to the ground,
Not even making a single sound.
Clara's amazed by what her friend has done,
Her friend the magical Nutcracker.

He takes her to many more places,
Where they meet many new faces.
Then she wakes up at a realistic size,
And she suddenly realises,
How real the experience seemed,
It turned out to be a dream.
But she is glad she experienced it
With her beloved Nutcracker.

Rebecca Oakes (12)
Burscough Priory Science College

The McCann Girl

You might steal a video
You might steal a television
You might steal money
You might steal a computer
You might steal an old lady's purse
But never ever a girl.

Who would kidnap a girl?
Only three at the time
Who would accuse the parents
And get away with the crime?
Who did it?
Nobody knows?

What does the future hold?
The McCann girl
Small and frightened
Will she ever return?
Is she still alive?
Nobody knows.

Why accuse the parents?
What have they done to deserve all this?
All this misfortune and lies
When will she be found?
Will she ever be found?
Nobody knows.

Finally the proof was found
The picture of the small blonde girl
Could it really be her?
The girl who has been searched for, for months
No! Who is the kidnapper?
Nobody knows.

Katharine Clieve (12)
Burscough Priory Science College

Hamilton vs Alonso

Hamilton in first
Alonso in second
2 points in it
Surely Hamilton must win it?
Britain desperately wanna beat Spain
So much it feels like pain
30th September
The Japanese Grand Prix
Can Britain's 'wonder boy' Hamilton
Race to take some glory?

The big day has come
The drivers line up at the start
Hamilton and Alonso
Competing like angry bulls
'Bang' screamed the start gun
This really won't be fun
The track eating away at the wheels
Every corner causes a thousand squeals
Can Britain's 'wonder boy' Hamilton
Race to take some glory?

10 laps to go
To lose would be a blow
He could see Alonso in front
He was catching him up
Ever so slowly pushing his luck
Then it happened
Hamilton overtook
He crossed the line, what luck!
Britain's wonder boy Hamilton
Had raced to take some glory!

Matthew Oshinowo (12)
Burscough Priory Science College

The Great Fire Of London

The Great Fire of London
The Great Fire of London
It was once there
But never seen again
The night came
The night there was a fire.

People running
People running
Running from what was coming
People scared, people hurt
Would it ever stop?
People scared, people hurt
Would people ever be OK?

The Great Fire of London
The Great Fire of London
300 houses burning burning
Nothing they could do
People wanted it to stop
But it just kept on burning.

The Great Fire of London
The Great Fire of London
The fire had stopped
People crying, people dying
The Great Fire stopped
It will never happen again
Or will it?

Oliver Cox (12)
Burscough Priory Science College

The Raging Fire Of London

It all started here,
Everybody full of fear
Where do we begin?
Maybe with the 300 houses being burnt down.

There's no dark
There's no silent
There's just death
People stepping into the heart of death.

Pigeons flutter
People bellow begin to stutter
'Lord what can we do?'
In hours the fire rages everywhere.

Raging roars everywhere
What should we do?
Shout help!
Call help!
What should we do?

Rebecca Winrow (12)
Burscough Priory Science College

John Terry

John Terry in his mask,
Playing tomorrow will be a task,
John Terry wants to play,
But the doctors want him to stay in all day,
John Terry is the best,
Better than all the rest,
Chelsea won the match,
But Terry's mask is still attached,
Terry will soon be fit,
With not a mask, not one bit.

Haitham Cherkaoui (12)
Burscough Priory Science College

Burscough V Boston

Burscough V Boston side by side,
They go for their warm up with a slip and slide,
The ref blows his whistle, we're ready to begin,
There's my favourite player Adam Flynn.

Back in for the team talk,
Out again with a smile,
Everyone's head up,
We'll win by a mile.

The game kicks off,
Boston are leading,
Not for long though,
Thanks to Cieran Killheeney.

Matt Parry goes down,
The ref's awarded a penalty,
Killheeney scores,
Full time, it's tea.

Jack Cosgrove (12)
Burscough Priory Science College

Exams

Oh no! Oh no! It's that time of year,
Exam time has come, it's finally here,
Feeling nervous, but looking strong,
You sit the exam, short or long,
Then you've done it, hoping you did well,
Results come back, you're feeling swell!

But the QCA think it's easy,
Will they make it harder? I'm feeling quite queasy,
I might not make the same good grade,
That I might once have made,
But I'll see it through, and try my best,
And try to succeed, just like the rest.

Alistair Nelson (12)
Burscough Priory Science College

The Game Of Few Sides

Hustle and bustle all through the town,
Everyone in sight heading to the ground,
Fans to the front of them,
Fans to the back of them,
Teams picked and players kitted,
And ready to go.

Koumas to the left, Valencia to the right,
The ball goes in the box, Heskey with the strike,
Siberski charging forward, crunching tackle last gasp,
'Penalty,' scream the fans, 'No,' says the linesman.

There goes the ref's blow,
Half-time here we go,
Heskey through, down falls the hero,
Piercing blow - penalty slow,
Dutch dynamo Denny places the ball into the net,
2-0 screams the followers onwards we go.

Super Sib bursting forward straight towards the gaping ground,
The ref's hand straight to the ground,
Super Sib stepping forward ready to take the penalty onward,
The back of the net it rumbled '3-0' screams the fans,
The ref blows, it's all over.

Hustle and bustle all through the town,
Everyone in sight, heading from the ground,
Cheers all round.

Kieran Heapy
Burscough Priory Science College

This Man Was A Great Man

Neil never got to hold his little daughter
But chose her name on the day he died
A musical man and loved to cook
With his frying pan.
Neil died of a heart disease
And could never rest with ease.
This man was a great man.

Friends and family took part
In a 90 mile walk in his memory.
He felt sick when he went on the ferry
He always dreamed of doing this walk
When he got a new heart
This man was a great man.

Whythenshawe hospital were very kind
He had a clever mind
The coast to coast walk was a success
But the men were very tired
With blisters and bruises
They came home
This man was a great man.

I cried a lot when he died
But I knew he was safe up above
He will always be in my mind
We will all miss this great man.

Eleanor McCombe (12)
Burscough Priory Science College

Navy

Derek Lam,
Spectacular satin,
Deep, inky, navy,
Fabulous fashion,
Uniform couture,
Its blue passion.

Chanel Couture,
Every season,
Complementing lemon,
Shopping reason,
Sapphire, silky satin.

Chic Chiffon,
Catwalk queen,
Evening dress,
Upcoming scene.

Every season,
Shopping spree
Go for navy,
Instead of black
Marc Jacobs,
It's coming back!

Beth Disley (12)
Burscough Priory Science College

Ghost Owl

Swooping low,
Over the snow,
With the wind on its wing,
And a twinkle in its eye,
Yours is a glory,
That will never die.

As dusk descends,
And the forest sleeps,
The owl sits,
Atop a tree,
Waiting, watching,
For its prey.

Silently floating,
Over a blanket of white,
Talons poised,
Ready to strike,
Breaking through,
The icy crust,
It scoops up a vole,
In its grip of death.

Adam Wilson (12)
Burscough Priory Science College

The Penguin's Dinner

As the aquatic and flightless birds waddled on,
The sun hardly shone,
As the penguins made their way to the sea,
You could hear their feet tapping like a woodpecker on a tree,
And they still waddle.

The penguins stopping was a mistake,
As the sea still looked like a distant lake,
They huddled up to keep themselves warm,
And they started to walk at the crack of dawn,
And they still waddled on.

They decided to toboggan down the hill,
And they all got another chill,
They all got up and the old oak tree,
And what could they smell but the salty sea?
And they still waddled on.

The penguins had finally reached the sea,
The penguins' faces were full of glee,
They started to jump for joy at their meal,
Full of tasty krill, squid and fish,
And they still waddled on.

Freya Ross (12)
Burscough Priory Science College

People's Princess

31st of August comes and goes,
People's princess among the olds,
Warriors, heroes, princesses and more,
Run into the arms of Death's galore.

Diana, Diana, why oh why?
That tunnel that night,
We wanted to cry.

Flashes of cameras,
Shouting of crowds,
Limousines crashing,
Cars bashing,
Darkness falling, all is lost.

1st of September sadness grows,
Everyone mourning for their girl,
For one who wore so many pearls,
For one who gave so much,
We're so sorry, we are,
You are our girl.

Running into the arms of death's galore,
People's princess dead for evermore.

Paige Fairhurst (12)
Burscough Priory Science College

A Crocodile's Dinner

Dangerous swimmer, silently glides
Through murky swamps.
He slides onto land without a sound.
With a snap at a deer.
Who was in so much fear.

He grabbed the deer with a flash.
Gave his tail a great big lash.
He rolled and rolled
And rolled with his prey,
Bones cracking on the way.

And then death.
The deer has taken his last breath.
Sharp teeth rip and tear.
Until the deer is no longer there.
The crocodile returns to the water.
At the end of the slaughter.

Arron Waggoner (12)
Burscough Priory Science College

Lava, Lava, Everywhere!

Spewing lava and ash they fled,
Volcano blows, eight dead.
Soldiers stationed alone as can be,
Running away and trying to flee.
Rescue ships scoured the sea,
Why, oh, why could it be me?

Two miles of lava along the floor,
Smoke engulfed their bases even through the door.
Debris spouting into the blackened sky,
Forty one live, as eight die,
The fire dies off, the smoke is no more,
There is nothing left but ash on the floor.

Jordan Freeman (12)
Burscough Priory Science College

My Parents

My parents are kind,
They are always on my mind,
They are always here for me,
Wherever they may be.

My parents comfort me when I am down,
And they make me smile when I have a frown,
They will never ignore me,
And always listen to me.

My parents will always help me,
Whatever it may be,
They take me out,
Without a doubt!

My parents are the best,
Even though I am a pest,
They are always helpful,
I will always be grateful.

Nikki Gibbs (12)
Burscough Priory Science College

Twinkle Ball

Twinkle house held their annual ball,
In The Lancashire Manor Hotel.
Event took place last Friday, for the Skelmersdale Charity,
For the twinkle annual ball.
The head of St Edmunds went on TV
David Ashley who sang Frank Sinatra.
Twinkle house said that they were well fed,
And stayed for the cazbar disco.
Dancing till late with someone to rate.
Having the time of their lives.

Amy Parker (12)
Burscough Priory Science College

Madeleine McCann

300,000, 300,000 money spent to find a child,
300,000, 300,000 a little girl so young and mild.
Maddie McCann left in hotel room,
Who would know it would lead to her doom?
300,000, 300,000 money spent to find a child,
300,000, 300,000 a little girl so young and mild.
'Find our Maddie!' her parent's plea,
At home with them they hope she'll soon be.
300,000, 300,000 money spent to find a child,
300,000, 300,000 a little girl so young and mild.
Private detectives search for Maddie McCann,
If they can't find her, no one can.
300,000, 300,000 money spent to find a child,
300,000, 300,000 a little girl so young and mild.
Many people think she's dead,
Her family hope not, yet still filled with dread.
300,000, 300,000 money spent to find a child,
300,000, 300,000 a little girl so young and mild.

Alex Bartle (12)
Burscough Priory Science College

My Poem

When the entrance song hits the fans are on their feet
When the bell rings, you can hear the fans sing
When the first punch is thrown you may be KO'd
When your opponent jumps off the ropes, you best think of a counter
When that counter connects you will have the advantage
When you hit your finisher that's it you may have won
When your opponent kicks out you release your anger
Then out of nowhere they hit you with a boot
1, 2, 3 the final bell rings and your opponent wins.

Andrew Bellingall (12)
Burscough Priory Science College

Save The Dolphins

Beautifully breaching, secretly sleeping,
When fishermen go hunting, dolphins go wandering,
They get caught in the nets;
Fishermen have all the sins,
Please save the dolphins.

Deep into the blue sea, beautiful creatures they be,
But danger is waiting, as they swim into the netting,
They haven't done anything, please save the dolphins.

Adopt from WDCS, dying dolphins will be less,
Dolphins could be saved, still splashing in the waves,
Buy the dolphin friendly tins, please save the dolphins.

Just make a small donation, we need the entire nation,
See them leap, smell the sea air,
Please save the dolphins.

Patsy Irizar (13)
Burscough Priory Science College

Christmas

Presents in sacks at the,
End of my bed.
I'm so happy with my presents,
Playing with the presents all day long.

Having Christmas dinner,
All I can smell is the turkey,
The carrots, potatoes, mash and gravy.

Snowflakes start to fall to the ground.
Everyone runs outside, into the snow,
All I can see is white everywhere.

A snowball hits my back,
It's so cold, throw one back.
I think to myself,
Christmas is the best time of the year.

Hannah McDowall (12)
Burscough Priory Science College

England 07

We achieved the glory in Sydney 03
Can we do it in France's Paris?
Against the Aussies we were in Heaven,
Let's repeat it in 2007.

France, Australia, we have beaten them all,
Let's just hope that our team doesn't fall,
With Jonny's kicks and Lewsey's try,
We beat the French, they wanted to die,
Pride, passion, belief and skill,
Unlike some others we've got the will.

We face the Springboks, let's hope they play poor,
36-0 doesn't matter no more,
The scrums will be tough,
And the tackles rough,
We will win every lineout,
To us this is our title bout.

We will win it nice and easy,
England's finest will make them queasy,
With the ball we will score a try,
South Africa will crumble like a piece of pie.

With Wilkinson, Robinson, Vickery and Co,
We will bring the trophy home,
Knighthoods and fame won't matter to them,
Just the medal will fill them with pride.

Callum Gamble (12)
Burscough Priory Science College

In My Box I Would Like . . .

In my box I would like . . .
Loads of money
Loads of chocolate
Loads of PSPs.

In my box I would like . . .
The 100m sprint
Loads of 42" TVs
Fifa 08.

In my box I would like . . .
An Xbox 360
The Champions League cup
All my best mates.

In my box I would like . . .
All my childhood memories
Everyone I've fancied
Loads of chocolate cake.

In my box I would like . . .
All the Monopoly board games
A gold Champions League medal
A Nintendo Wii.

In my box I would like . . .
The biggest water park in the world
The Liverpool team
Call of Duty 3.

Ben Dreha (12)
Burscough Priory Science College

Excellent Everton

Brilliant goal,
Makes the Red side sigh,
Brilliant goal
Makes the roars of the Blue side go sky high.

Excellent miss,
Makes the Red side sad,
Excellent miss
Makes the Blue side shout how they're so bad.

Brilliant goal,
Means the Blues are on a roll,
Brilliant goal,
Means the Red side need to get a goal.

Excellent miss,
Makes the Blues want to diss,
Excellent miss,
Makes the Red side wonder how they missed.

Thomas Anderson (12)
Burscough Priory Science College

Her Sunflower

Standing tall, it blew in the silent wind
Watched by a young schoolgirl, whilst gardening
Inspired by the 15ft friendly creature
She desperately longed to have her own feature.

So she planted a seed and waited for it to grow
Her hopes of a 15ft creature to show.

Standing small, it grew in the warmth
Watched by a schoolgirl, it began to form
Inspired by her feeble creature
Her love was great for her 10inch feature.

So she looked after it with love and watched it grow
Her hope for her 10 inch sunflower that showed.

Emily Baldwin (12)
Burscough Priory Science College

The Dance Show

My foot started tapping,
As the music began to play,
The atmosphere was buzzing,
I'd been looking forward to today,
Everyone was dressed up,
In their very best of clothes,
All I could smell was the perfume,
And see their feathers and bows.

The children started dancing,
In their little skirts and tights,
With big smiles on their faces,
They were lit up by the lights,
They danced upon their tiptoes,
And twirled around with glee,
The mums and dads were smiling,
This is what they wanted to see.

The music changed to modern,
And now there was a chance,
To see the boys and girls together,
They were going to do break dance,
They walked on with lots of attitude,
And spiky coloured hair,
The clothes were big and baggy,
And their tummies were all bare.

The last dance of the evening,
Was the old style cha cha cha,
It brought back lots of memories,
For the grandads and grandmas,
The audience was clapping,
And they got up from their seats,
They loved to watch the dance shows,
It was one of their little treats.

Natalie Eccles (12)
Burscough Priory Science College

Madeleine McCann

Off to Portugal
On a plane
Away from England
And the horrible rain.

A week of sunshine
And topping up the tan
Building sandcastles
Will be Madeleine McCann.

One day at a hotel
Mum and Dad are getting tea
Madeleine has gone missing
Where can she be?

Everyone searched for her
Even the hotel manager John
But they could not find her
Madeleine was gone.

Is she still alive
Or is she dead?
That poor little girl
Who was snatched from her bed.

If you know where she is
Bring her back if you can
Where are you now
Madeleine McCann?

Georgina Fairclough (12)
Burscough Priory Science College

My Friend Vicky

My friend Vicky is very strange,
She runs round like a chicken,
But I hope she'll never change.

She makes me laugh,
When she acts so silly,
But that's a good thing,
When it's chilly.

If you ever meet her,
You won't stop laughing,
She can make anyone smile,
And the audience keep clapping.

Her dark brown hair,
And very tall figure,
She's just as bouncy as
Disney World's Tigger.

Her large brown eyes,
Must hypnotise,
And her smile's so huge,
It reaches to the skies.

But most importantly,
She's a very good friend,
And no matter what
That will never end.

Jenny Donohue (12)
Burscough Priory Science College

Memories Of The Night

Haunted by the screams of my nightmare in the light,
Faces of sheer terror roam around in my mind.
People crying carry their sadness with me all day.
The constant murmurs make sure it's peace I cannot find.

A mocking silence comes when all I want is sound.
The remnants of my dream make tears prick my eyes.
That nightmare's screams and events I wished not to see,
Stay with me forever until it's hearing I despise.

My day to day battle with life is long and everlasting,
Dragged down by colours of anger and sad.
The ongoing flashes of envious green and furious red,
The colours of emotions, so hectic, so mad.

My eyes droop as my life is reigned by memories,
Memories of the horror of a dream so foul.
I wait for the memory to fade and be forgotten.
I wait until I hear that final terrified howl.

Isabel Bryant (12)
Burscough Priory Science College

Claude's

I never need an excuse to visit Claude's, one of my very favourite
restaurants,
And with news that has splendid church town-based establishment
Has just unveiled its latest lunchtime and evening menus, I'll be there
Like a flash and I'll pick up the phone and order a bacon butty,
What I like about Claude's is its total dedication to providing diners,
With delicious and memorable dishes, they really care about food,
And it shows when your meal is presented in an imaginative and
stylish way,
And the taste is amazing! Regular visitors will notice the restaurant
Has just been tastefully decorated and now boasts a new heating
and air conditioning,
Which means you will dine in a nice, warm and cosy atmosphere
At this time of the year, and stay cool in the summer.

James Byrne (12)
Burscough Priory Science College

Rhys Jones

A boy, a child, whatever you like,
Went riding one day on his bike.

With one intention on his mind,
To look to search and in the end find.

A knife, a gun, whatever it takes,
A feeling inside much more than hate,
Imagine that feeling when he tells his mates.

He found the car,
He wanted to harm more than a scar.
The people inside talking away,
Too far to hear what they had to say.

A boy, a child, whatever you like,
Walking home from football early that night.

Thinking about his birthday and what he might get,
A new mobile his mind was set,
And the tunes he would be able to get.

A hoodie on his bike,
The gun ready to strike,
He pulls the trigger at the car,
After all it's not very far.

The bullet, the noise, the sound,
It was the boy's head in the end it found.

Two boys, two children, whatever you like,
One dead son,
One on the run.

Two parents, sad, lost and alone,
The other too scared to phone.

How do you get over your son?
How do you get over knowing that your son had a gun?

Two families torn,
By children that had not long ago been born.

Jessica Linford (13)
Burscough Priory Science College

My Liverpool

Liverpool are the best
They thrash the rest
The city is fantastic
The people are great
The offices give people their lunch breaks.

Everything inspires me
When I reach Anfield Road
It reminds me of memories.

The city is reaching new heights,
It's the capital of Culture 2008
The new buildings are massive,
So what do you think?

But all for one,
Not any of the people are gone,
Champions of Europe five times,
Couldn't get any better.
Liverpool.

Ryan Dobney (13)
Burscough Priory Science College

Pink Foot Geese

1 and 2 and 3 and 4
How about a million more?
Squawking loud up and high, looking at them makes you sigh.
They dive down like a grey waterfall
Come for the comfort and the food, they take farmer's carrots
Which is awful rude
As they fly so proudly and elegant above our heads
The sound of them annoys us in bed
But we love them so that we forgive them
In Martin mere is where they make a den
1 and 2 and 3 and 4,
How about a million more?

Heather Liggett (12)
Burscough Priory Science College

Madeleine McCann

Madeleine now has gone for month and day,
Now everybody is worried and in haze,
Everybody seems to care,
Thoughts are there for her everywhere,
Not a single day goes by,
Where she has gone, and why?
Let's hope she will be safe and well,
Instead putting her parents through hell,
People are looking around,
Hoping Maddie will be found,
Mum and Dad have visited the Pope,
To give a glimmer of hope,
This is a very scary time,
We should wish it will be fine,
We can only hope and pray
That Maddie will return to her family any day.

Louis Nelson (12)
Burscough Priory Science College

Reward For Maddie

Caught amid the crossfire of blame
Can't you see that she is in pain?
Lost her daughter five months ago
Please help she is only 4 years old.
All this is doing is causing aggravation
They have spent £300,000 in investigations.
All the rumours that have been going round
People saying she is dead.
Family hope not dead but they are filled with dread
There is a reward of £100,000
We hope she will be home with us soon.
Private detectives search for Madeleine McCann
If they cannot find her no one can.

Emily Peel (12)
Burscough Priory Science College

Guess Who?

To name all the things that she's good at,
Would take me 3 years and a day,
I'll tell you a few of them now,
And I hope that you'll have time to stay.
She's kind and caring and helpful,
She helps me up when I am down,
Never makes you feel blue or sad,
Makes you smile when you can only frown.
She makes you feel happy and jolly,
Takes you out at the weekend,
Let's you have most things that you want,
She'll care for me forever till the end.
There are lots more things that she's good at,
But these are all I'm going to name,
Just to say that she's the greatest,
And I pray that in your family you're lucky enough to have
one the same.
Have you guessed who it is yet?
Go on have you guessed?
I knew you'd get it, my mum, Lesley,
She's simply the best.

Kerry Wilde (12)
Burscough Priory Science College

One Courageous Man

Martin Luther King was a courageous man,
A man who believed in a free world,
A world where people won't be judged by the colour of their skin,
But beneath the flesh.
How can people think above others?

Martin Luther King was a courageous man.
He fought a war,
A meaningful war,
One in which many had followed his teachings.
He never asked to be thanked for what he did,
He never stole,
He just fought for what he believed in.

Martin Luther King was a courageous man,
He inspired many civils as a preacher,
His legacy lives on through the world.
People now see there are not coloured and white,
There is just one race, the human race.
In the end he lost his life for the people,
A sacrifice that shall never be forgot.

Ryan Lee (12)
Burscough Priory Science College

Good Old Ted

On the 29th of September
Ted's heart stopped
It was a sad thing to remember
For four minutes it stopped beating
For David, Lynne, Joanne and Victoria
The pressure was heating
And as anxious Beckham dashed from LA
There were only a few words to say
'I am sorry Dad!'

Victoria told David
'Don't blame it on yourself,'
But Becks couldn't stop thinking
About good old Ted's health
David was like a little lost lamb
Joanne, Lynne and Victoria were doing the best they can
Different rumours we constantly hear
Let's all hope Ted pulls through clear.

Tom Wright (12)
Burscough Priory Science College

The Falling Man

I'm standing at the window; I don't know what to do,
People I know are screaming, I think they feel the same way too.

I keep on looking down, my vision is very blurred.
My skin is starting to blister with the heat of hell in here.

My mind is working overtime; it's time for my final prayer,
Take care of my wife and kids as long as I'm not there.

My heart is pumping faster as I take my final step.
1, 2, 3, I'm ready to leap to my eternal death.

Craig Shaw (13)
Burscough Priory Science College

School Fight

'Someone's going to be killed,' shouted those surrounding
The two boys fighting like in a boxing championship
They glared at them through their camera phones shouting, 'Kill him!'
60 seconds of the fight posted to You Tube on the night
The head teacher soon came round but then unfortunately
Saw a crowd and said,
'Mobile phones, in this case, usage goes far beyond this place.'
Entertainment, so it was called
And through the rumours we knew it was cold
School fights have always been there
But nothing so cruel
And definitely not cool,
'Someone's going to be killed,'
Shouted the surrounding
As the chilling playground filled.

Matthew Abernethy (12)
Burscough Priory Science College

Sad Moments

On the way from football practice,
A young innocent child stops at a car park in Croxteth.

He's playing around with his mate,
Not knowing he might be bait.

Bang, bang, bang guns go up,
Bang, bang, bang, he goes down.

Shooter scatters quick and fast,
Now he's gone, time has passed.

We hope he is ashamed and does come forward,
For he is the one with the guilt to carry.

They're tracking him down day by day,
Please come in,
That is what we say!

Elliott Howarth (12)
Burscough Priory Science College

Linnets On Form

Booth, Booth,
Played the ball,
Killer picked up and skinned them all.

Killer broke free,
To a knock on the knee,
Pulled the trigger,
And it bounced like a flea.

Goal, goal,
Killer scored,
Burscough leading,
And now they're bored.

Wait, wait,
Flynn's gone down,
It's a pen,
Boston's keeper looks a clown.

There's the whistle,
It's all over,
Burscough through,
And now to play Dover.

Josh Hall (12)
Burscough Priory Science College

FA Cup Glory

At the Bamber Bridge
There was a war
Burscough V Boston ended
With a brilliant score.
Boston scored,
They were in the lead
A goal for Burscough
Was all they need.
The 76th minute lead
They didn't stand a chance
But then Burscough scored
And then they sang and danced.
Burscough was thrilled
They weren't in danger any more
If Burscough could hold on
They could just last for a draw.
But then surprise
Burscough was in delight
Another goal was scored
And Burscough won the fight.

Matthew Goodyear (12)
Burscough Priory Science College

Gone And Never Seen Again

One night she went.
Five months on she is still gone.
Is her body in a fridge
Or is it on a mountain ridge?
Do we know?
No one knows!

Is she dead
Or is she not?
If she is dead how did she die?
Was it an overdose
Or did she just get murdered?
Do we know?
No one knows!

Who took her?
Did her parents kill her?
Or did she just die by accident on holiday in Portugal?
Do we know?
No one knows!

Sam Stringman (12)
Burscough Priory Science College

Gone In 38 Seconds Flat

7 years gone and the girls reunite,
Sporty, Baby, Posh and Scary,
Also Ginger together,
On a cold winter's night.

Fans registering with text and email,
Receive message that tickets are on sale.

Trying to get tickets,
Everywhere is jammed,
Time is running out,
And the lines are still jammed.

Finally got through,
But now there's the waiting,
Nervous and excited,
And slightly anticipating.

Suddenly all sold,
The tickets have gone,
In just 38 seconds,
There was left with none!

Charlotte Randall (12)
Burscough Priory Science College

Guy Fawkes

A dragon's den, a camper's tent
But Guy Fawkes went to Parliament.

He walked inside
With oil by his side
Down the stair
Below the king he went
Pouring oil all over the place, he lit a match and dropped it
Just like that.

A dragon's den, a camper's tent
But Guy Fawkes went to Parliament.

At the door
A man stood tall
Looking straight at him
The man walked in and started to shout
'Hey you put that fire out!'

A dragon's den, a camper's tent
But Guy Fawkes went to Parliament.

The next morning he was taken
To the tower as dark as night
Blood on the floor where he was walking
Came to halt next to a man who was holding a lever
He pulled it and Guy started to fall
Crack the deed was done.

A dragon's den, a camper's tent
But Guy Fawkes went to Parliament.

And now we sing that we still had the king
After that great but terrible day
The song is sung to this day
And will be sung for evermore.

Elliott Powell (12)
Burscough Priory Science College

Football

Football is very good,
You should play it, yes you should,
All the players playing their game,
If you don't play you're in shame,
The special goalkeeper saving all those shots,
Strikers not saving but scoring lots.

Football is very good,
You should play it, yes you should,
Trying hard to get your goal,
Play football, it's in your soul,
Once you're winning, you're in the game,
You're the best of them all.

Football is very good,
You should play it, yes you should,
It's nearly game over, defend, defend, defend,
You win and you are legend,
The time nearly up there, waiting for the whistle,
Getting excited, they are so really tired.

Football is very good,
You should play it, yes you should,
Finally there goes the whistle,
The time has come to thank the other team.
Walking off the pitch slowly, time to celebrate, approaching
The changing rooms, *wow,*
Shouting and screaming, that they had won!

Philippa Boulter (12)
Burscough Priory Science College

The Twenty-20 Cricket World Cup 2007

The Inaugural Twenty-20 Cricket World Cup
Exciting till the final ball
Got off to a fantastic start
Gayle hit a century, he sure played his part
This century would prove to be,
The first and last amazingly.

The highlight for all
Yuvraj Singh hitting 6 sixes
Off only six balls
Fielders to the right of him
Fielders to the left of him
The crowd went wild
The ball hit a child
Stewart Broad was bowling
The ball wasn't rolling
Flying out the ground like a rocket into space.

The next stage was the Super eights
Which brought in tremendous gates
England were rubbish
India were great
South Africa had won but it was too late.

After the Semis
The finalist would prove to be
India and Pakistan
Pick a winner but don't ask me
The finish was tight
With India victorious
I'm sure you'll agree the tournament was glorious.

Matthew Birchall (12)
Burscough Priory Science College

Poor Little Hedgehog

It was the dead of the night,
Nothing to be seen
Then a noise scared the life out of me,
What was it?
I don't know
But a hedgehog
It was!

Then the lights down the road,
What was it?
Move hedgehog,
But so slow.

Worrying what to do,
Move out the way little hedgehog.

I run and run,
But nowhere to be seen.

It's safe, the car has gone
The hedgehog is safe,
And it is so late!

Sophie Tams (12)
Burscough Priory Science College

My Hero, Owen

This is a poem, about Michael Owen,
Injuries he's had, one, two and three,
One to the head, and one to his knee,
The third one, to his groin,
That seems to be torn.

Injury after injury to the Toon hero,
The mighty has fallen as the pain is never-ending.
What can he do to strengthen his walls?
It's like he is standing in front of a locked door.

Euro 2008, is such a long wait,
Before are the qualifying games,
England is the name
'Is Owen ready?' asks Captain John Terry.

Dean Ashton is his substitute,
Although it is not definite that he will be used,
Hopefully Owen will be back and fighting,
With Heskey in the starting line up.

Jessica Riley Green (13)
Burscough Priory Science College

Bluetongue

My cows cannot breathe,
I just can't believe,
That these midges can cause this,
Bluetongue disease.

My cattle are dying,
And I feel like crying,
My bills I cannot pay.

We have had foot and mouth,
Floods, now bluetongue too,
Is it time to give up farming,
Because I don't know what to do?

Goats, sheep and deer too,
This bluetongue virus,
Is out to get you.

With Defra restrictions from farm to farm,
We can just hope and pray, bluetongue,
Doesn't cause too much harm.

Lauren Forshaw (13)
Burscough Priory Science College

Poor Little Dolphin!

One little dolphin,
Washed upon a shore,
Hearing his sad baby cry roar,
Hoping someone would hear him cry, he let out a little sigh.

In his dying voice he said,
'I wish I could snuggle up in bed.'
Poor little dolphin all smothered in red,
Covered up to his little head.

40,000 gallons of oil,
He was like a big massive ball,
It turned out to be carbon monoxide,
A deadly killer made by man.

No one heard his cry for help,
He was trying his hardest just to yelp,
Poor little dolphin ended up dying,
So everyone ended up sad and crying.

Hannah-May Rothwell (12)
Burscough Priory Science College

Helping A Friend

Helping a friend,
How could he know this would be the end?
Only his friend could see the end.

Splash! As he entered the pool,
The thugs were fools,
He clung to reeds,
As he began to bleed.

Stone after stone
Brick after brick,
When would it end?
Wondered his friend.

He tried to escape,
His friend was too late,
Drained of energy,
He let go and sank to the depths below.

Helping a friend he now knew this was the end.

Adam Swift (12)
Burscough Priory Science College

Guy Fawkes

There 'twas a group of thirteen,
Had just finished their teens,
They planned a blast,
So it would last,
They thought they would run out of casts.

One sent an anonymous letter,
He thought it was all for the better,
They've had killed the king,
His glass eye would have gone ping,
There would be nothing left to find.

The letter reached the king,
He went ting,
The king made plans,
He gathered his clans,
And went to stop the gang.

Tom Lowe (12)
Burscough Priory Science College

Last Lesson

As I sit here in my seat,
I chew the end of my pen,
The teacher's writing something,
About numbers one to ten.

When suddenly the bell goes
I swiftly pack away,
Clatter down the stairs,
That's it for another day!

Ellie Jones (11)
Central Lancaster High School

Cinderella

When Cinderella thought that's it
'I do all the work while you just sit!'
She exclaimed loudly.
The sisters sat there sipping lemonade that was cloudy
'When my day is done
I hope there will be sun
So you will be hot and sweaty!'
Of course the sisters were horrified when they heard what she said
And they went straight to bed!
One day there was a ball
So the sisters went to the mall
They stayed there all day
Without a delay.
They came back and found out they shopped
Till they dropped
The big night came
Cinderella said it was lame
The sisters were off in a tick
And their dog called Mick
Was really a fairy godmother!

Billie Collins (12)
Central Lancaster High School

I Am Evil

I am the darkness leading you away
I am the thoughts that lead you astray
I am the one thing that gets in your way
I am your conscience.

I am what makes your stomach turn
I am what makes your heartache yearn
I am from what you learn
I am your guilt.

I am your vengeance
I am your desire
I will be your remembrance
I will be your fire.

I will be your only thought
I will be what you have bought
I will be what you have brought
I will be your liar.

I will be your deceit
I will be below your feet
But you and I will never meet
For I am evil.

Mark Dandy (17)
Holy Cross College

A Daughter's Sonnet

You're a mean Mum,
A suffocating, smothering, safety-mad,
Sad, no-risk, no-fun, no-life Mum.
Why can't I go out with my mates?
What's wrong with this skirt?
It's fashion, not a belt.
And who are you to talk?
You're a whining wino, an alcofrolic,
What's a shot between friends?
You're Strictly Come Dancing, I'm strictly Skins
Let's face it, we're different, we're not joined at the hip
I'll pierce my lip, if I want to
I'll be who I am, whatever you think . . .
But can I just borrow a tenner?

Catherine Rawsthorne
Holy Cross College

Why Do We Kill For Fur?

The moon was out, the stars were bright
It was a very warm spring night
I looked outside and what did I see?
A deer passing by from me.

It was a very cold and frosty night
I was holding onto my covers tight
There was a bang of a shotgun
Suddenly
Looked outside and what did I see?
A deer *dead* in front of me.

Why do we poach animals why do we kill?
Even when these animals are nearly extinct we do it still
What is the meaning of this just for a fur dress?
If we carry on poaching animals,
This world will be in even more of a mess!

Emily Shrimpton (11)
Ingleton Middle School

In The Magical Garden!

In the normal garden,
I found a big surprise,
I opened the big brown, varnished door,
And opened up my eyes!

In the magical garden,
With trees so tall and green,
The great, tall trees like oak and beech,
Were gazing down at me!

In the magical garden,
I think I'll stay the night,
But now I'm getting hungry,
I think I need a bite!

In the magical garden,
I see the sun rise,
Up and over the big, big hills,
This is the best surprise!

In the magical garden,
It's nearly time to go,
I'll really, really miss this garden,
Especially the melting snow!

In the magical garden,
I start to hear my sighs,
I pull the big brown, varnished door,
And open up my eyes.

In the normal garden,
The children at the park,
I hear the birds all singing,
Kites, starlings and a lark.

Rosie Louth (11)
Ingleton Middle School

The Lonely Lantern

Their only light is the lonely lantern
As they staggered after their only hope
Cursing the rocky, rutted ground
After the lonely lantern they grope.

Some twenty-four there were tonight
All unaware of the other
Blood dripping from deep cuts and wounds
One after another.

The lonely lantern coaxes them on
The only light on that dark night
The misleading, unknown stealer of lives
Tempting the vulnerable after the fight.

Souls that were once beautiful like flowers
They thrived on happiness and joy
Now stripped of everything but pain
Suffering, grief, regret and toil.

Rags hanging off blood-soaked arms
Ripped and torn with age
I'm tired of the anguish of this sight
Young men trapped in an invisible cage.

Their hearts screaming to be let out
But their minds; shut in forever
Locked in a cage of memory
Evil, cruel memory, drenched in terror.

All I can do is stand and watch
A punishment for sweet bravery
Tasting that bitter taste of hate
For the Devil's lantern, the lonely lantern.

The light of death and the map of pain.

Sarah Atkinson (12)
Ingleton Middle School

Autumn Air

When a traveller goes by,
And feels the touch of autumn leaves,
Only rough air greets him.
He does not feel wanted anymore,
Yet, the chirping birds carry him on
And he huddles along,
Almost in a graceful way.
The silver grass does not whisper,
But stares plainly
As if wanting to know more
About the musty smell
Which has overpowered him.
Leaves have turned ill,
And fall to an unknowing ground,
Which is new to them.
Suddenly the traveller falls,
And summer is gone.

Ruskin Fox (11)
Ingleton Middle School

The Midnight Sky

See the stars at night
They're all twinkling brightly,
What a lovely sight!

The moon is glowing
Meteors are showing up
The sun is sleeping.

Shooting stars fly by
How I love to see the night
It is in my dreams.

Beautiful black night
I look to be reminded
Of the midnight sky.

Rachel Fulford (11)
Ingleton Middle School

Hallowe'en

The demon's face was covered,
With a black hood and cloak.
It was Hallowe'en,
Its main aim to provoke.

Children were playing,
So engrossed in their game.
Did not notice the figure,
Who to their side came.

The boy's eyes grew heavy,
His skin grew white.
As the mysterious demon,
Walked into the night.

The very next morning,
When the child awoke,
And to his horror,
Found two bites on his throat.

Charlotte Taylor (12)
Ingleton Middle School

My Generation

What reputation has my generation?
Why should we be caught up in the violence?
Hoodies, tracksuits guns and knives,
These horrible things are not a part of my life.
Drugs; not my thing, drinks of coffee can do the thing!
They think they're all bad but all they are is blooming mad!
Robbing shops, stealing cars, taking a butty from a butty bar.
Gosh, I hate my generation
All I want is peace, no war, no thieves just peace and no more
That is what I want for *my* generation.

Andrew Walker (13)
Ladybridge High School

My Generation

I've seen nothing of the world
Or set paw outside of this alley
I don't know if it's concrete
Or perhaps a wooded valley.

I dare not go out
What cruelty does the world hold
I have to cower in the back street
Probably until I'm grey and old.

I've only laid eyes on one human
Grumpy, angry, two-legged and tall,
Who threw me out here, all alone
So I wonder, are there any nice humans at all?

I just faintly remember the past
Living with my mother and kin
Warm, sheltered, fed and watered
Now I'm lucky if I find an over-turned bin.

So I'm dull muddy brown
And I'm not pure-bred
My eyes are two different colours
Does that mean I'm better off dead?

Thinking of life and what it gave me
I wonder what else has to live like I do
Outside in wet and dry, hot and cold
Spring, summer, autumn and winter too.

What is the purpose of life
With the misfortune it brings?
If strays like me are useless
Do I count for anything?

And now I wonder
With a horrific sensation
Is it just me who lives like this
Or my whole generation?

Sarah Wagstaffe (13)
Ladybridge High School

Talkin' 'Bout My Generation

Imagine a bright world for the future
Where conflict and bombings do not exist
Where the impossible problems have been solved
Just imagine you can't resist.

Imagine a bright world for the future
Where beautiful animals breed to make new,
Where people lead a peaceful life
Imagine the future, it belongs to you!

Imagine a bright world for the future
Where people do not live on the street
The world's budget will be higher
There's a place for you in the future - take a seat!

Aaron Unsworth (11)
Ladybridge High School

My Generation

Maths, English and science too
All the subjects we have to do
We love them, oh yes we do
Even when we haven't got a clue!

Education is the way to go
Teaching is everything we need to know
For in the future we take our stand
We could be the leaders of this proud land.

My generation is misunderstood
Television shows teenagers all covered in blood
But my life is different I'm happy and free
Which is what my generation wants to be.

Charlotte Sleigh (12)
Ladybridge High School

School Or Holidays?

Why do we have to go to school?
School is boring,
We just sit there in silence,
A big book with loads of page
And all I can write is a couple of sentences.

Why do we have school holidays?
School is fun,
We meet up with mates
And have a good gossip.
There's so much fun to do!

School! School! School!
School's not important to me
I'd rather meet up in clubs,
There's much more fun there
And in school you have to do work.

Holidays! Holidays! Holidays!
Holidays are not important
We are better educated in school
And education gets you a better job
To people that like school, like me, not you!

Mariam Khan (13)
Ladybridge High School

My Generation

Texting or talking, what will I do?
Homeless or rich, which will it be?
Street or mansion, where will I live?
Optimistic or pessimistic, how will I feel?
Reviled or prestigious, how will I be seen?

Shabana Bholat (13)
Ladybridge High School

My Life

I remember when I was thirteen
Very tall and full of calcium,
All because of Dairylea spread
Spread on my butter and bread.

I think that cigarettes should be banned
And all the litter on the land.
Every person who is a criminal
Should be treated like an animal.

Why has the bus fare changed?
Seventy pence had been arranged.
Why, fifty pence was just fine,
Who agrees with this poem of mine?

My life is what this poem's about
Make things better people, shout!
Help all the people on the planet
That is my message for all who want to hear it.

Ashley Walsh (13)
Ladybridge High School

My Generation

My life in my generation
Is scared and frightened.

No good behaviour
No helping old people.

I have lots of things to come my way
Although it will go fast I will enjoy my day.

Thugs, guns, drugs and violence too
My loving family will get through.

Murder, suicidal and accident who
That is my generation.

Jazzmin Horrocks (12)
Ladybridge High School

Learn More About Football

Football is the best sport going as it keeps you healthy and fit,
Learn new skills and discover things about football, bit by bit.
Wake up in the morning and get those legs going
And soon, without noticing, you'll start scoring.
Going to Old Trafford is every Man Utd fan's dream
As the whole stadium echoes as the fans chant and scream.
If you want to become a player like Ronaldinho
Practice and increase your speed and soon you'll be like Robinho.
The Red Devils are just the best, no matter what people say
They'll chant and kill anyone, any day.
Our rivals and enemies Chelsea are so easy to beat
The fans can't be bothered getting up off their feet.
With goal scorers like Carlos Tevez and Ryan Giggs
People should learn to stop smoking and leave those cigs.
With a player like Paul Scholes with so much power
He can destroy anything, even Blackpool Tower!
So are you ready to watch football and learn?
Because soon it will be your turn!
Have you got what it takes?

Shezad Karim (13)
Ladybridge High School

My Generation

My generation is really bugging me
And as a result my life is awfully frustrating.

Living on the streets
I have my eyes on the world.

People have money to waste (I don't)
They buy new phones and top brand clothes.

I don't like rubbish on the streets I've got to live on them.
I bet they don't do it in their home
So why do it in mine?
No one will give money
Even though I see them with posh stuff to decorate them.

Steven Thompson (14)
Ladybridge High School

My Generation

M y name is Chloe Molyneux
Y our name might be Joe Smith but there are . . .

G angs, guns and drugs around. In the newspapers
E verywhere there's things like violence you never see anything
that is good in the papers, do you?
N ever quite my things I do because I can be good and I can be bad
E ven though you never seethat side
R especting everyone and everything
A nd walking down the road on my own looking at the violence
and the kids that bully
T alking and giggling that's what I do with my mates
I love to spend the time I have with my mate but sometimes
O n my own, it's alright too
N othing in this world would change me because I am what I am.

Remember, you're only a child once!

Chloe Molyneux (12)
Ladybridge High School

Non Discrimination Glasses

One day I wish for the world to make something amazing and useful
Something that could still make people in a wheelchair look beautiful.
Also to stop people staring at them on the sidewalk
Instead with this creation, everyone will get to talk.

Something to keep the world together, so no matter who you are
Everyone will feel as one forever
And no one will think of anyone else differently.
Instead they will all get together disabled or not
and get along constantly.

So I thought of a brilliant and fantastic thing for all lads and lasses,
And they are, non discrimination glasses.
And this creation will make the world a better place to be,
For everyone, my family and me.

Tom Ingram (13)
Ladybridge High School

My Generation

My friends call me cool
'Cause I've got a big pool.

My brother loves music
He's starting to lose it.

He acts like a hoodie
But is allergic to chuddy.

My sister is my twin
Helping old people like Jim.

She puts them in the pool
And they all sick and drool.

But last of all my mum and dad
Listen to old music, so sad!

They think that I'm weird
Even though Dad's growing a beard
And that's *my* generation.

Danielle Sherwood (12)
Ladybridge High School

Different Things

My friends might dress different
You're not trying to connect.
Gangs and wars but that's not me
Everyone is thinking different.
Never are they right
Every day is worse than the last.
Running from police which they are wrong
Anywhere I go there are different people.
Turning every corner, but there is no escape.
Isn't there an answer to all this madness?
Only I know the answer,
No one else does!

Matthew Fish (13)
Ladybridge High School

My Generation

M oney all the time
Y outhful

G ood behaviour
E njoying
N aughty
E verybody doubts me
R aving lunatic old people think
A lways trying to impress
T ension around crowds
I mpostor to older people
O pportunities not always coming my way
N ot always trying my best.

Mitchell Dougill (12)
Ladybridge High School

My Generation

M y name is Kasam Khan
Y oung and very fashionable

G oing to school
E very day cause mischief
N ever daydreaming
E ating my lunch
R eading my books in English
A ssembly
T alking to my friends
I ntriguing
O n top of the world
N o more to say.

Kasam Khan (13)
Ladybridge High School

Rubbish On The Street!

I wish I was a person
So then I had a mouth!
If this came true
I would have something to say.
There are bins about
So why dump on me?
When I get full
Why do you all complain?
You all call me trampy
All I want to know is why?
It's all your fault
I'm the way I am
If you took more care of me
Then I would be clean!
I'm only a street,
So why call and trash on me?

Lyndsie Chorlton (13)
Ladybridge High School

My Generation

My generation is full of games
Staying in rooms all day long
Drugs and drink not surprising anymore
Cars and football is it all
Every Saturday will be it
Sitting at home, bored.

Mate knocks on
I go out have a kick about
Have a laugh
It's not all bad
Chillin' on the street
Talking about who to meet

We're not the bad kids on the block.

Dominic White (13)
Ladybridge High School

Talkin' 'Bout My Generation

In my generation . . .
We do what we are told
We have lots of responsibilities
Though many things are sold.

In my generation . . .
We don't get enough money
But we have a good time
Lots of kids go off and smoke
But one day they may choke.

In my generation . . .
There hasn't been a war
Though I heard there were two before
I don't think there should be any wars
Because some people don't want more.

In my generation . . .
People will cry with hearts of thunder
While others will wonder and wonder.
What a generation
I wouldn't want to miss.

Praise Phiri (11)
Ladybridge High School

My Generation

My generation is great and fun
Chances come and go
But there will be more
Some people like sport and others like books
Some people are tall and others are small
But we're really all the same.

My generation is fun
My generation is happy
My generation is the best.

Rory Litler (12)
Ladybridge High School

Parallel Happiness

In this world full of madness
There is one lonely girl
Trying to express her sadness.

Indeed she believes in happiness truly
But there is one thing standing in her way,
That horrible bully.

Locked behind the bedroom wall
She's dreaming of somebody that she could talk to
Or maybe just a best friend to call.

Even though dreaming is just an illusion
As she cries herself to sleep
She's thinking about the conclusion.

When she saw a brand new day
A smile appeared on her face
She took a stare at her new house, where she's now going to stay.

Those shining lights of crossing cars
Showed her the way how to start the life again
And now she can see how she's the brightest out of all the stars.

Being clever, pretty and smart
Forgetting about the past, she found the love of her life
Which mend her little heart.

He taught her how to live her life
Flying on the wings of love
After years, they became husband and wife.

Aleksandra Gesicka (13)
Ladybridge High School

Why Do We Commit Crime?

Why do we commit crime?
These yobs, murder, drink and take drugs,
Think they're hard, dressed like mugs,
Huddled in gangs then end up behind bars.
Do they care? I don't know.

Why do we commit crime?
Thieves, shoplifters, smugglers and all,
Why do they do this? I don't know.
Make a fool out of their lives,
Do nothing for a living.
Earn, live a luxury life, have a family and a few kids.
Do they care? I just don't know.

Why do we commit crime?
Lying, backbiting, stealing all count as a sin.
Get rid of the habit, but how?
I don't care, but do it.
Why do we do it?
Why? Why? Why?

Why do we commit crime?
How do I get control of this world?
I wish it were a better place,
Can we do any better? I don't know.
Why do we commit crime?
I don't know but I wish I did.
Why do we commit crime?

Hannah Khan (13)
Ladybridge High School

Orphan Child

I look up to the bright white sky
As the rain splashes down on my face
It feels like acid sizzling down
With aching pains in every limb.

I hear glasses smashing, people arguing
I look around the empty street and see it's just inside me,
I try to think of happy times, those everlasting memories
Suddenly they're blackened out by fear and reality.

I know this pain will never go
It may get worse for all I know.
Can no one else feel this but me?
This painful heartache, tearing me down.

I start to read a creased up letter
The sun begins to shine much brighter
In our family portrait, we look pretty happy
Now there is no family our portrait can no longer be.

I open up my big black door
Where once before lived a family.
But this I come home to every day
This is my life, my shelter some days.

Nazish Razaq (13)
Ladybridge High School

My Generation

T errible teenagers roaming the street
E ven in the day and night drinking in the week
E very day hanging with my mates
N ever going home till very late
A lways looking very cool
G anging up on the little fools
E veryone having a good time.
R aving so much, yes we shine
S o now we have finished it's time to go but tomorrow's another day,
yes and no.

Chloe Roberts (12)
Ladybridge High School

Smoking

Why do people smoke?
If smoking's not healthy and smoking's not big,
Why do people take the risk of destroying all their lives?
Will people try and quit or will they carry on and even then put
other people's lives at risk as well?

Why do people smoke?
You are damaging your lungs and destroying all your body
And do you really want lung cancer for the rest of your life?
You are waiting a long time, hoping that someone generous
will come along
And say that they will donate you a lung.

Why do people smoke?
Do you really want to damage all your life
Or will you be big and brave as a lion to turn around and say
that you will stop?

Why do people smoke?
I don't really know why people want to smoke but one day
we will find out
Why people want to still sit around and just destroy all their lives.

Lorna Barnes (13)
Ladybridge High School

My Generation

A door is a simple object that opens and closes.
The person who walks through that door, that's what's important.
At first the baby in his mother's arms warm and protected
For in those arms he will come to no harm.
Next a child playful in nature running around
No care in the world, not ready for what next he will become.
Then a teenager bashing the door open
Playing his music, calling his friends rebelling against authority
Pushing his luck all the way to the end.

James Leach (12)
Ladybridge High School

Talking 'Bout My Generation

We had a mum once
She loved us and cared,
Then one day they took us outside
And left us to die.

Me, Tommy and Cleo went hungry
And started to shiver.
Our bodies only two weeks old,
Our innocent little lives flowing down the drain.

Until one day a light shone through like the sun,
A smiling face answered our cries,
We were taken away into the warmth
And given back our lives.

Now we are grown-up
And have a family who love us,
They play with us and feed us
And keep us safe when danger comes.

Olivia Bailey (14)
Ladybridge High School

What You Have To Do To Be Me

I am young
With a big tongue
That talks for hours.

I feel like a fool
Because I hate the pool
I know I've lost it.

But it makes me sick
I know its thick
But that's the way I am
So put a sock in it 'cause I know you can.

Tasnia Islam (12)
Ladybridge High School

My Generation

My generation is full of drugs and crimes
Not enough justice to solve the lies.
Hoodies and gangs roam the street
While old people try to sleep.
Late at night vandalism grows
Graffiti spreads, gangs begin to grow.

My generation is not like that
I'm not the one you think is a brat.
Leave me alone, I'm not the one to blame
I'm not the one who should take their shame.
If you ask me it's the parents fault,
Shabby upbringing and nasty faults.

Leave me alone, I'm not that bad,
Stop calling the cops, it makes me mad.
Me and my mates, we like a laugh,
We don't go out to make folk sad.
Some people think we are all the same,
That's not true; we are not *all* to blame.

James Aspinall (13)
Ladybridge High School

Litter

Litter, litter everywhere
On the floor or in the air.

Litter makes the streets look messy
So pick it up and don't you be messy.
Litter makes me feel very sad
And makes me really mad.

It injures innocent animals
So please, just listen to my advice
Help the environment today
Pick up your litter every day
And put it in a bin!

Paula Parkinson (14)
Ladybridge High School

Talkin' 'Bout My Generation

I'm talkin' 'bout my generation
Where we use phones for communication
Nobody will commit suicide through depression
In this world today people use cooperation
But will this happen in the future I wonder.

Through the eyes of a doctor
It is said I am never a loner.
Through the eyes of an orphan
I am not allowed to be free.

The future is different
Technology will be important
There will be cars that can fly
Later on, children won't cry.
I'd like peace and,
Harmony will take place.

Mithun Kerai (11)
Ladybridge High School

Talkin' 'Bout My Generation

In the future we'll run out of oil
There will be war and the sun will boil.
In the future we'll live on Mars
We'll have floating buildings and have hover cars.
Nowadays the world is simple with a lot to do
There is so much in life
The whole world is ahead of you.
The world is full of different people
Some rich, some poor, some blind.
But underneath everything we are the same
And so is everyone you can find.

Henna Hussain (12)
Ladybridge High School

Untitled

Having more freedom
Is the door to paradise.

Doing as you're told
Is the path of a good future.

Having fun
Regretting what you've done.

Having no responsibility
Is a bad place
Having responsibility
Is a good place.

Having wars underneath the dome
Wishing I was at home.

The earth is collapsing
The earth is warming.

Having more planets
Having more animals and humans.

Having less planets, having less animals
And having less humans, having more war
Now the world has ended.

Seeing people who are blind
Doing what they don't mind
Sharing their feelings
Making less dealings
Nowadays the world is simple
Nothing much to do
Wishing there was much to do
The world is full of sparkles
Glitter falling down from the sky
But now the world has ended.

Aaisha Sarwar (12)
Ladybridge High School

My Generation

Do you ever question why we are here?
Is it a money fight for survival or is rich or poor fighting for a place?
Do disrespectful, trouble makers, lazy people fill this world
Or is it just posh, talented, money-making people?

Have you ever wished you could change the world?
We look around from time to time
And think how much better the world would be if a few things
were different.
Maybe you'd see the end of poverty and war.
We'll shout it out but who will listen?
We always know that our parents will listen
But our parents can't stop poverty and hunger, can they?
You speak the words because nobody else will.

Holly Farrell (13)
Ladybridge High School

Through The Eyes Of The School Walls

I can hear the voice of students and teachers
The whispers of the secrets and things I just can't say.
I can smell the food of cookies from the kitchen.
I can smell the food from the dinner hall and in the staffroom
the cups of tea.
There are displays and posters all around the corners, the new TVs
are watching me.
I see all I need to see.
I can feel lively or lonely.
I am touched by the students.
I live in the heart of the school,
Home sweet home I say.
What am I? The school walls!

Dominic Barlow (14)
Ladybridge High School

Life Of The Unfortunate

To change the world I'd like to do
Just to show how lucky are you.
To see the lives of the unfortunate out there
And try to make some people care
To see their faces and how they react
And to realise what a big impact
They have on them but don't realise
To see the sorrow and hear the cries
And people live their lives without knowing
The ignorance that they are showing.
Tis sad to see just how they suffer,
Some kids without a father or mother.
It's a struggle to get through the day
With no one listening to a word they say.
Begging for help, pleading for attention
All they want is love or affection.
All the things that you possess
And you live your life in happiness.
So next time you're feeling down,
Sit back and take a good look around
And realise your life ain't tough
Compare to some you have more than enough.

Shelby Heaton (14)
Ladybridge High School

One Day The World Will Come To An End

One day the world will come to an end
The trees will snap,
The ground will crack,
Children will be crying,
People will be weeping,
The planet will be rumbling and crumbling,
Buildings will be shattering,
People will be screaming, running,
The world will come to an end.

Ibrahim Patel (11)
Ladybridge High School

In The Future

In the future
They could invent machines that can make you fly.

In the future
There will be life on Mars and we will discover new planets.

In the future
The world will run out of oil and we might come to the end of the world.

In the future
There should be animals that can talk all the different languages.

In the future
They might invent new hover cars and gadgets in cars.

Rebecca Flatley (11)
Ladybridge High School

Is It Love?

From the beginning we were friends
And now I tell him love never ends.
When I fell for him that's when I'd never love another
We cried, we laughed and often did cute photographs.
I love you
I told him I loved him, and he told me back
Then he said, 'Jess I feel for you and I want it two last'
We remember the good times that we had
Once again, I'll tell you that
I love you bad!

Jessica Mayhew (13)
Ladybridge High School

Orphans

How did I get here?
Born by a woman drinking beer
Left in a box never to be found
Left all by myself upon the ground.

Homes and homes I got sent
But only once I got fed.
My first foster family was quite rich
And once a week I washed my own dish.

Clothes and shoes were rubbish and ripped
People laughed as they pinched and ripped
I am an orphan
Please try and foster me.

Kirsty McCabe (11)
Ladybridge High School

Gunshots

We are so lucky we get food and water
People in Africa, Iran and Iraq
Hardly get to eat and have bony feet
And are always sweeping their dirty floors.

Babies are born anywhere
In the garden, in the house or even in the middle of the street.
Babies cry when they get hungry
But what can we feed them?

Babies scream to fulfil their dreams
Mums and dads, nowhere to be seen.

Huzefa Patel (13)
Ladybridge High School

Generation

We are a generation -
But who knows why we're here?
What is a generation?
Say it loud and clear.

Laziness, leadership:
If that's what it's all about?
Silliness, stewardship
Say it to us; make sure you shout.

Make it stick in our mind,
So we know what to say when you ask.
How do you know and what did you find?
Or are you hiding behind your mask?

Is it fiction or is it fact?
Or is it just something that you believe?
Maybe it's just a massive act;
In the future we could be deceived.

None of our generations are the same;
It doesn't matter if you're young or old.
Each one has an individual game -
Your generation can never be sold.

Is yours about music or is it dance?
Or are you in a magical land?
Do you live with Prince Charming in romance?
What about on a beautiful beach covered in sand?

In the future will it still be the same?
What will happen when we go?
Will all the places have a different name?
Well, we'll never know!

Faye Wright (13)
Ladybridge High School

Talkin' 'Bout My Generation

Talkin' 'bout my generation
To make me get a better reputation.
There should be no depression
And there might be no pollution.
More animals, more animals,
There should be more,
To make them together and furthermore
The budget will be higher,
I'm not a liar.
Global warming, carbon emissions,
No CO_2 and greenhouse too.
Peace 'n' harmony is gonna come to life,
No more bombings.
Dangerous drugs will be reduced,
Then drunk people will not be produced.
No bad people,
No bad people,
That's more like it.
That's better and everyone will like it.
If you can change everything around,
There would be a better ground.
There should be no drug dealing,
If you do, it would make a bad feeling.
There should be no hustling,
Especially no gambling,
No more crimes to be done,
Without this, it would be more fun.
To make me get a better reputation
This is talkin' 'bout my generation.

Naim Ismail (11)
Ladybridge High School

Talking About My Generation

Talking about my generation,
Who knows what it is all about?
We are the kind of nation
If you know scream and shout.

Talking about my generation,
Will our music be the same?
Or a brand new recreation?
Maybe it will be the same?

Talking about my generation,
All the gadgets that have been created.
They'll probably make a new PlayStation -
Or maybe one day they'll all be hated?

Talking about my generation,
What is your favourite thing?
Football, dance, your biggest sensation,
You'll never know what it could bring.

Talking about my generation,
Now we have cars, planes and buses.
Before you had to go to the station,
Nowadays no one cares or fusses.

Talking about my generation,
Tell me is yours boring or fun?
Mine is great, it's all about fashion.
Has your fun even begun?

Talking about my generation,
In our schools we have loads of lessons
We learn maths, English, science, German
RE, PE and how to make a cushion!

Talking about my generation,
We take many trips all over the world.
Egypt, China, Spain, hardly ever Britain!
Places like out of a dream world.

Talking about my generation,
What was it like in the past?
They were the kindest of their nation
Come on - we'll find out fast!

Eleanor Wright (13)
Ladybridge High School

Talkin' 'Bout My Generation

Sun shinning brightly,
Slowly tanning the people,
They are feeling great.

Winds are beautiful,
Swaying flowers in the breeze,
Petals falling off.

The winds getting fast,
Branches fall off the high tree,
Leaves fly all over.

Tornado coming,
Whirling, whirling all around,
Hide in your homes, quick!

Hide, hide for your lives
Hide in your home and beware
It's coming closer.

Run, run from the winds
Faster, faster, it's coming
Hurry, run faster.

Quick, run, it's coming
Argh!
Oh no, it's got you!

We need to take care
The environment won't last,
That is my last word!

Jai McCabe (13)
Ladybridge High School

My Generation

This generation of 2007
This generation living in Heaven.
All we do is chill all day
We get bored, we go out to play.
We have too much new technology
So say gadgets to pass time
But even with all this
We still have so much crime.
The past generations they had no TVs
No mobile phones or Nintendo Wiis.
And what about the future generation?
Will they also be living in Heaven?
Will they be as lucky as me?

Bilaal Mangera (13)
Ladybridge High School

I'm Homeless

I, me, I'm homeless
Leave me be, I'm homeless.
Sad, alone, by myself.
I'm not mad, but I am sad.
I'm hungry, I'm starving,
Help me to survive.
How do you expect me to live?
I'm homeless, help me,
I'm homeless.
I want to live but not like this
I want to eat chocolate, be warm and have company
So, help me, help me, I'm homeless.

Chloe Cleary (11)
Ladybridge High School

My Generation

Music, drugs, knives,
Youth negative vibes.
Guns in the pocket of little kids
Everyone terrified of the street
Now is the time to make my stand
A single voice in a crowded land
Real life that's what this is
A child at school that's what I am
Tiny children that act lie children
Into reading and writing
Other kids like me never answer back
Never hanging around on the streets
or in the back of street cars.

Sabahat Hussain (13)
Ladybridge High School

My Generation

M ost people don't understand
Y oung people and all of their plans

G enerations change, so do ideas
E verybody's different and so are feelings
N ever underestimate the power of will
E very child knows what I mean
R ather than talk they bottle it up
A fter every sentence they say but
I gnorance is bliss
O ver the years
N obody knows how much the generation
can change.

Becca Hardman (13)
Ladybridge High School

My Generation

My generation
Here's what it's about
My generation
Let's scream and shout

My generation
Dance or sports
My generation
We can do allsorts

My generation
Are we the same?
My generation
Or are we all in a game?

My generation
Ten or thirty-five
My generation
Let's dance and jive

My generation
It's all cool
My generation
If you follow the rule

My generation
Has yet to arrive
My generation
Is down my drive

My generation
Fun and boring
My generation
Let's get scoring

My generation
Old or new?
My generation
We all can argue

My generation
Forty or ninety-five
My generation
Has yet to survive

My generation
It's just around the bend
My generation
It's come to an end.

Sian Alldread (13)
Ladybridge High School

With No Characters

Live life to the full,
You cannot write a story
With no characters.

What am I here for?
What is it, life just simple
Just something we lead?

Sometimes I feel like
Life, is a yarn of cotton,
Never seems to end.

I wander alone free
I see the clouds above my head,
They are all like me.

There is no one here
No one to bug and annoy
But this is not life.

Friends, that's what life is,
Stories never seem to work
With no characters.

Adam Settle (13)
Ladybridge High School

Talkin' 'Bout My Generation

Look at those hips, the eyes, the hair,
Look at those lips, the thighs, the stare.
They're pretty, they're cool, they're my generation,
They're the ones who misinterpret our nation.
Laughs and giggles through the day,
Killing them unknowingly as they pray.
For hope,
For faith,
For their opportunity to shine.
Get a ticket and wait in line
Without the looks, dreams, make-up too
There'd be nothing special about you.
Beauty's not in your appearance or figure
In fact, it's something so much bigger.
With meaning,
With light,
Minus the fight!
It's simple, it's pure,
It values something so much more.
Beauty lies within the holder,
It's larger, deeper and much bolder.
So young girl, dry your tears away
Along will come a brighter day.
Your eyes will shine and your smile will glow,
You're beautiful in everyway you should know.
Be yourself and set yourself free
For you're the most beautiful person you could ever be.

Laura Horne (14)
Ladybridge High School

Nothing Will Change!

A dark thick mist covers the land
Small quick flashes of light piercing the darkness.
Bangs and clicks echoing through the silence
Just stage one in survival.

Emerging through the mist and silence
Armies of men and machines
Metal birds and beasts surround
Stage two now to begin.

Stood praying, waiting, I wouldn't fall,
'Now!' called the men.
The moment had come
Now to leave freedom and enter war.

Entering the fire, leaving the peace
The only safety and protection
My small, metal beast
Ambushed by men, vision of death.

Lifting my hands hearing a click
Memories of past, seeing what's near
All colours fade, join to one
Blackness, surrounds, no sounds to hear.

A new day dawns
An old one fades
Visions of future
Nothing will change.

Ben Hunt (13)
Ladybridge High School

My Best Friend

You are friendly, kind and caring
Sensitivity, loyal, and understanding,
Humorous, fun, secure and true
Always there, yes that's you.

Catching my tears when I cry
Pulling me through when the tide is high.
Standing by, all the way
Here to help me through the day.

When I am worried you give me hope
When I am confused you help me cope.
Of all the friends I've ever met
You're the one I won't forget.

We're friends at school
I'm tall, you're small.
But we're the friends at school
That we're the best of them all.

Olivia Penn (12)
St Bede's Catholic High School, Lytham

Menagerie

It's cold and wet, slithery too,
But not too small to strangle you.
It's long and thin but can be fat
But not too hard to gobble you back.

It's small but wise, with big fat eyes,
That dozes through the day,
If you ever see it at night,
Beware from night to day.

It's small but fat with a fluffy back
That hops throughout the day.
It's cute and small but can stand tall
Forever and a day.

Sarah Barnes (12)
St Bede's Catholic High School, Lytham

Stormy Night

It was a dark and stormy night
It gave me such a fright
When I watched its terrible might
I got very scared!

When the lightning was in the sky
I looked at it and said, 'Oh my!'
It was enough to make me high
I got very scared!

Then the thunder made a boom
I ran upstairs to my room
I didn't want to be in a tomb
I got very scared!

The rain nailed the roof of my house
I hid myself like a mouse
Not worrying about a woodlouse
I got very scared!

Sam Jones (12)
St Bede's Catholic High School, Lytham

My Generation

M usic and iPods,
Y ouths and gangs.

G adgets and gizmos,
E lectronics and games.
N ineties and noughties,
E mails and Facebook.
R ockets to space and
A irports expanding.
T ravel to places both near and afar,
I nternet usage and high mileage cars.
O rganised lives and diaries so full,
N o time to be children our lives never dull.

Rachel Pendleton (11)
St Bede's Catholic High School, Lytham

My Generation

Twelve is the age to be,
There's lots to do including TV.
There's gossip and friends,
Phones and trends,
Twelve is the age to be.

Twelve is the age to be,
There's loads of fun including you and me.
There's fun and games,
There's school and mates,
Twelve is the age to be.

Twelve is the age to be,
There's loads of school which can sometimes bore me.
There's books and bags,
There's homework and tasks,
Twelve is the age to be.

Twelve is the age to be,
There's loads of people who I love to see.
There's my mum and dad,
My nan and grandad,
Twelve is the age to be.

Hannah Woods (12)
St Bede's Catholic High School, Lytham

Games Of The Generation

I have a Nintendo, I hit the power switch,
the sapphire-coloured dragon flies around the screen,
it roars like a lion showing its fire breath.
When I play the game it transforms me into a young boy,
shooting arrows, using a sword to kill monsters,
with magic at the end of my fingertips.
I would rather play on my Nintendo
than a chess set any day.
Technology turns faster than the Earth.

Bradley McLaughlin (11)
St Bede's Catholic High School, Lytham

Do They Care?

Nurses and doctors rushing around
Bandages scattered all over the ground.
MRSA swoops through the air
Doctors and nurses, do they care?

Injury and illness, needles and pain,
People are starting to go insane.
Families of the patient are worried spare
Doctors and nurses, do they care?

Medicines and splints, injections and drugs,
Why can't they kill these dreadful bugs?
These patients are ill, this is not fair,
Doctors and nurses do they care?

The tiles are filthy and the beds are not clean,
The health care assistants are not nice, they're mean!
The hospital service is starting to tear,
Doctors and nurses, do they care?

Claudia Fiddler (13)
St Bede's Catholic High School, Lytham

Mummy, Don't Hurt Me!

Look at me Mum, what do you see?
Someone sad, hungry, dirty or do you simply not care?
I wish you would love me, it's just not fair.

How can you not see my tears
Or have you just drunk too many beers?
Why do you hurt me, why do you swear?
Why won't someone hear my prayers?

All I want is to be able to play
Have friends and toys and somewhere nice to stay.

I want to be free Mum, can't you see?
The person you hurt the most is always me.

Kayleigh Wainwright (13)
St Bede's Catholic High School, Lytham

Hi-Tech Life

The film rolls over happily
Spreading on a blank screen
Enjoying a fun ride
Up and down the projector
Like a Ferris wheel
People come and go
To enjoy the show
But the good life does not last forever
He will soon be gone
And stored in a dark closet
He enjoyed his time at the amusement park
Until he had to leave into the dark
He was bought by a nice man
Who also owned a horror film
They made friends and enjoyed another ride at the amusement park
He was taken to a shop
He changed
He got more high tech
Just like his friend
They were played on Callum Comp
He didn't last long
He was sent to the dump
With his favourite song
Then came Larry Laptop
He was a good friend but not the same
They could not keep up
He was top of the range
But was a pain
All they wanted was their main
Callum Comp's at the dump again.

Matthew McIlwham (13)
St Bede's Catholic High School, Lytham

My Generation Poem

My name is Joe
I ain't got no ASBO
Yet, but I have got a pet.
Her name is Puss
She makes such a fuss.
I got a mobile phone
It's called a RAZR
But my dad says it don't look like a shaver.
I have a PSP
If I've been bad my mum takes it off me.
I've also got a PS2
But you can't play that when you're sat on the loo!
Hoodies and bling are the must-haves
If you want to be one of the chavs.
Grandad says you should be proud of your nation
I say, 'No Grandad, that's *your* generation!'

Joe Bolton (11)
St Bede's Catholic High School, Lytham

Willow Tree

I'm the willow tree in the park
That nobody sees in the dark
I see things that I can't prevent
Like bullying, drugs and drunken rants.

I twitch and shudder
At the words that they mutter
They make others cry and tease the ones that are shy
I close my eyes shut so I don't see what they do when they're drunk.

I see the children play
And sadly I know that one day
They might be like this, drunk and violent.

Megan Phillipson (12)
St Bede's Catholic High School, Lytham

Generation

Engines roaring like a lion,
Exhausts chugging past,
Bangs as planes fly overhead,
The odd whirring of cogs in faulty vehicles.

In this generation many strange noises,
Loud vehicles storming past.
See cars and buses everywhere,
Ubiquitous, no avoiding them.

Aboard a bus, I'm deafened.
Centuries ago - no such thing as motorised transport,
Amazing how things change,
Wish it hadn't, it's smelly and muggy.

Cars pass,
Polluting, exhausting, fast,
Cheetahs into the distance,
Still they come, wildebeest in a stampede.

They have these things called aeroplanes,
Rocketing overhead.
Travelling so quickly,
In a second they're gone.

Solid traffic's the worst of all,
Raging drivers vociferate, swear, gesticulate.
Reverted to cavemen in a minute.
The cars move, the drivers are human again.

Trains, more advanced now,
Gone from beauties to beasts.
Hardly any steams now,
Used to love them, how my views change.

New generation's gone mad,
Zebra being chased by a lion.
Transport, hanged our world forever,
Never to be peaceful again.

Engines roaring like a lion,
Exhausts chugging past,
Bangs as planes fly overhead,
The odd whirring of cogs in faulty vehicles.

Gregory Young (12)
St Bede's Catholic High School, Lytham

The Computer

I'm constantly making noises
Being shouted at
And then I get sat on
By a big tabby cat

Mum says I'm useless
Dad says I'm great
Just because through me
He got his first date

I go to bed when I'm told
I wake up when I'm needed
Once I didn't wake up
He hit me, he did

Once awake
I an sometimes snooze
Just like Dad
When he's had too much booze

I am constantly
Giving them advice
But they ignore me
Now that's not very nice.

Luke Houghton (13)
St Bede's Catholic High School, Lytham

It's So Unfair

I used to live in a horrible home,
I was left all alone.
I was only eight weeks old,
I was always freezing cold.

They never cleaned my cage out,
They never let me run about.
I escaped one dark dull night,
That gave them a terrible fright!

Now I'm here at the RSPCA,
I'm here every single day.
I only want an owner
So I am not a loner.

I am so much happier now,
How could anyone be so men, how?
By the way my name is Bopsy
I am ever so cute, will someone adopt me?

I'm as fluffy as a teddy bear,
I also need lots of care.
My ears drag along the floor,
They sometimes get very sore.

My fur is as white as ice,
I am very kind and very nice.
I hop around like a kangaroo,
I will always be a friend to you.

Daniella Boyce (13)
St Bede's Catholic High School, Lytham

Talkin' 'Bout My Generation

Fashion is ruler
Fashion is king
With fashion you gotta have everything
Talkin' 'bout my generation

There's guns
There's war
Everybody gives to the poor
Talking' 'bout my generation

People who are gay
Always get a say
Talking' 'bout my generation

Anorexia, not eating any food
Obesity, eating too much
And being very rude
Talking' 'bout my generation

Plane into Twin Towers
Bombings on the tubes
Terrorism is pointless
Talking' 'bout my generation

Drugs are no good
Crack, cocaine and ecstasy
Child and animal cruelty
Talkin' 'bout my generation.

Tom Hornby (13)
St Bede's Catholic High School, Lytham

Iraq

Bang, boom and crash!
That's all I hear nowadays.
I loved the little camp at Weeton
We practiced and trained hard there,
I knew what I was in for,
I thought it wouldn't hurt
But I'm here now.

My tent is a sauna;
All hot and stuffy.
My heart is beating like a drum,
The guns are like daggers,
Pain in their chest,
I know now it hurts,
I can't go back.

On the battlefields
The sand crunches below me;
Like crisps being eaten.
Gunshots deafen my ears,
Bombs rumble the ground;
Like an earthquake.
My life is wasted here.

My body is like jelly,
My eyes are bulging,
Can't bear to watch the deafening destruction.
One by one, down they go,
Like dominoes in a row.
Enemies, colleagues and friends,

With a gun in my hand I advance,
The sounds in my ears
My head and heartache,
What's that all about?
The crowd roar in anger
Like a mob of angry men.
Can't they see we are here to help?

An ambulance rushes past
Nearly sweeping me off my feet.
There lies a bloodied body,
Oh no, it's John Paul!
His body lies damaged,
Smashed like a pane of glass,
I hope he will live.

It's nearly time
I want to go,
Can't wait till Christmas,
I need not fear,
I'll be home soon . . .

So he said.

Leah Roberts (12)
St Bede's Catholic High School, Lytham

A Musical World

Although we don't notice,
It is everywhere.
For music is a part of us
We would never forget.

How could we live without it?
Imagine how that would be.
A world without music
Could never really be.

As you can see
The world lives musically.
Show, classical, pop or rock,
There's something for everybody.

It's like water,
A necessity.

Helen Sleeman (13)
St Bede's Catholic High School, Lytham

Hi-Tech

You cannot see me
Or be me
Believe me
Relieve me.
You can never leave me
Since your world is full of life
My world is just 3-D.
You're totally in control of your ICT
You never see that you need to let me be.
I long to be free
Not taken for granted,
Like a seed freshly planted.
Where would you be without me?
There are millions of you
But only one of me.
I will stand out in the crowd
Like an endless sea.
Everywhere you look,
Everything you see is me.
Even when you go to the movies
Who's the actor that nobody sees?
Me, the star of every show
But who would know?
I'll give what's needed, night or day
But it's taking its pay
But you know what they say
Though I don't rest at the end of the day.
But who cares what I feel
To you I'm not real.
I know the things you conceal
And I hope that you know
One day I'll go.
When I go fast everything else will be slow.
When your world rocks and will become a wreck
But that's what you get when you mess with the hi-tech.

Niall Shepherd (12)
St Bede's Catholic High School, Lytham

War In Iraq

We went into war on that fateful day
Who knows we could have to stay
It is deafening when we hear that sound
And then to see men fall to the ground.

It is sad that men die
And you know that their families cry.
It is happy when you see air support
The courage of those men who fought.

It is good that I am here this day
To fight for my country for little pay.
At home my family will be proud
To see me walk through the busy crowd.

I do not brag that I'm alive,
I am just happy to survive.
I do agree I want victory
But all I want is to see my family.

Connaugh Daley (12)
St Bede's Catholic High School, Lytham

Skies Of War

War at sky, war on the ground, war all around.
Crowded places, silent in others
People thinking about their brothers.
War's not that good, sometimes it happens
Some people die, some people survive.
From swords and chains to guns and grenades
From bow and arrows to missiles.
War to war.
I wish, I wish, there was peace in the world,
I wish, I wish, the war was gone,
I wish, I wish, they'd get rid of the bomb.

Robbie Jordan (12)
St Bede's Catholic High School, Lytham

Guns And Violence

You think it's no big deal,
But violence is real.
From people fighting
To young children fighting for their lives.

If you're on the run with a gun,
Adrenaline pumps through your body.
You think you're cool
But you're the fool,
When you shoot someone in the head
And they are dead.

For what you think was right
Prepare to fight,
Because gun violence is at the top
And it *must* stop.

To stop gun crime
Now's the time
Before another young child dies.
It should make people upset and think
And look around at what has happened.
To enjoy lives and not take
But is the time to stop gun crime too late?

Thomas Malley (13)
St Bede's Catholic High School, Lytham

Why?

Wandering the streets at night
Trying their best to start a fight.
Guns and knives,
Take people's lives,
Why they do it isn't known.

Hearts as black as coal
Thoughts pounding through their head,
If they didn't see sense now
Someone else could be dead.

They didn't mean to do it
They thought it wouldn't hurt.
She was Daddy's perfect angel
And Mummy's precious girl.

Fear in their eyes,
Why didn't they see sense?
Waiting in the police car
Filled with anguish and suspense.

The little girl didn't pull through,
Her family now distraught.
The government need to know about this
Because knife crime needs to be fought.

Sophie Lowe (13)
St Bede's Catholic High School, Lytham

I'm Not Hungry

I look in the mirror
I see myself as fat
Each day I count carbs
And saturated fat.

My friends say I'm skinny
I believe it's a lie,
My mum says I must eat
Or I will no longer be alive.

My ribs stick out
Like branches of a tree,
Why am I so fat?
Why me, why me?

I'll starve myself
Until fainting point,
I go as white as a ghost
Then wake in my bed.

But still no food,
Just water then bed.

I sit in my room
And cry all day,
I know I should eat
Or I will pay.

My dad makes me sandwiches
I cannot decide,
Should I eat them
Or will I die?

What is happening to the world?
Will this change
Or will we go through
This hurt and pain?

Bethany Seed (13)
St Bede's Catholic High School, Lytham

Through Weapons' Eye

All you can see red,
Everybody is dead.

Slingshots into guns
Arrows to bullets.
Bed of blood lying on the floor.
Looking round and seeing much more.
Dropping bombs over cities
Blowing up houses
What a sight,
What a fright.
Like a vicious killer
Preparing to strike
Hiding in a dyke
All you can see red,
Everybody is dead.

Imagine blowing up a house,
Or even killing a mouse.
It's horrible to think
Bombs, grenades, tanks, rockets,
Bazookas, machine guns,
All these have a link,
Change!
A long time ago
They had none of these weapons
All except a minor slingshot
Or a bow and arrow.
All you can see, red,
Everyone is *dead!*

Sam Boardman (12)
St Bede's Catholic High School, Lytham

This War Is Never-Ending

Death and destruction
We feel it all around.
Giant destructive bombs
Exploding on the ground.

This war is never-ending
We can't seem to stop and look
At all the death we caused here
And people's lives we took.

We made our mark on people,
By making them afraid.
We should all just look now
And see what we have made.

This war is never-ending,
It will stay here till we die.
We should look and stop it
Not let life pass us by.

James Hardwick (13)
St Bede's Catholic High School, Lytham

Footballs

Footballs, footballs in the sky,
Footballs, footballs are sky high.
George Best, Ronaldinho and the rest,
They try so hard to win the test.
And to score and score some goals
And the rest they slide and dive
And then again they score 5!
They hit the post - that they hate the most
But they try and try to win the most.
Even though they try so hard
Knees are as muddy as a farmyard!
Sometimes they win, sometimes they lose
But here we are, playing the beautiful game
And starring in the fame.

Harry Borman (11)
St Bede's Catholic High School, Lytham

Food Poem

Here I am staring at the mouth-watering pizza
It's covered with tasty yellow cheese
I grab it with ease

I'm so pleased
What a nice crispy crust
And I'm gonna eat it all, yes I must.

Pizzas have not been around forever
So I wonder what my grandfather ate
I bet it was a plate of dates.
Now that my meal is over
I need to sit down and digest
Tomorrow's tea, maybe I should suggest.

If I could have my favourite meal
A Chinese would be first on my list
Definitely a meal not to be missed.

Johnathan Knight (12)
St Bede's Catholic High School, Lytham

Car

It growls louder and louder,
3, 2, 1, *go!*
It jets off into the dusty distance,
like a blur of colour,
like a cheetah amidst the orange desert,
a trail of fast wind passes by as it does,
blowing dust aside as though bowing before it.

As it moves through the tunnel,
it growls, echoes through the tunnel like a crowd cheering it on,
its engine revving more and more,
the finish comes into sight,
the golden banner breaks as it passes through,
it's won the race.

Sharn Farazian (13)
St Bede's Catholic High School, Lytham

Reaching For Stars

In the beginning we saw
Looking up to the sky
Reaching for stars
Trying to understand

We tried to explain
So myths were created
Stories were told
But we wanted some answers

Is there someone
Looking down
Watching us
Guiding our way?

But without any proof
Nothing was certain
Still looking up
Staring in wonder

Until one day
We saw much further
Proof was given
Questions were answered

New worlds discovered
Some larger in size
Far, far away
Impossible to reach

Our picture not complete
We wanted to explore
New transport was invented
We could travel great distance

Now up there
With no peace or war
Many more answers
Creating many more questions

When will we stop
Or even slow down?
Will the truth be told?
Will we ever know?

Until that day
We carry on searching
One after another
Reaching for stars.

Bethany Rigby (14)
St Bede's Catholic High School, Lytham

Temptation

I look into the window,
I have seen things I like.
A pair of sunglasses and denim shorts
I start to have many thoughts.

Should I buy them for summer
Or should I save up?
I have bought a lot today
But my temptation won't give up.

I walk into the shop and see many things
Tops, jeans and diamond rings.
Many shops many trends
But this is where I want to spend.
Pick up the clothes I like
And take them to the till
Like chocolate I think they're brill.

I walk out the shop
Glad I bought those clothes
What I buy next,
Nobody knows!

Lauren Doddemeade (13)
St Bede's Catholic High School, Lytham

The Oldest Football

I'm the oldest football in the Manchester United store room.
I've only been played once this year,
When I played it was a dark gloomy day like me.

But today I'm getting played
I'm in the centre of the pitch.
It's halfway through the match now
I've been battered and bruised.

Bang! I'm in the net 1-0 to Man U
Rooney's boots are as yellow as lasers.
Ronaldo as fast as a cheetah
The team are a lot faster than the ones who kicked me back then.

Wow! Look at Rooney's boots and Ronaldo's
They're as light as a feather.
The ones when I used to play were as heavy as a TV.

And it's the end of the game, 1-0, Man U
One of the most brilliant games I've played in my life
And one of the last!
Now I'm back in the store room waiting for another game!

Lauren Gallagher (12)
St Bede's Catholic High School, Lytham

Family

The youngest in my family is my sister Victoria and she is the loudest
Then it's Craig and he thinks he's good at everything
Then Harry who gets in lots of trouble
Then Albany who has just left school and is starting college
Then Bobby who has just got a dog
Then Kelly who has got a baby
Then Darren who I don't see much because he is in the army
Then my mum who is strict but can be very nice as well
Then my dad who takes me out everywhere
Then John, he got married to my mum last year
Then Phillippe who is very kind and that's my family, it's very big!

Jason Naylor (12)
St Bede's Catholic High School, Lytham

Rugby

I am soaring through the sky
He jumps up and grabs me.
I am pressed into his red and white jersey
And then all of a sudden
He kicks me!
Rolling and rolling,
Not stopping,
Like leaves getting blown by the wind.
I get picked up and then
Crunch! I am flying through the air like a bird.
I hit the floor and stop dead.
A red and white jersey jumped on me
A loud high-pitched sound goes off,
I hear screams of joy start.
I am placed on a piece of plastic,
I feel leather hit me in the back
And I go flying through the post.

Jack McGuinness (12)
St Bede's Catholic High School, Lytham

Space

In the 50s people only dreamed of going into space
They just looked up to the sky and said, 'Wow!'
Now it's reality, new solar systems, animals in space
If you said that in the 50s people would say you were crazy

Burning stars float in the sky
The moon is there as well, moving the tides
Planets are there, like neighbours on a street
All the planets have visitors, maybe even us
But we have not discovered them

Rockets as big as skyscrapers shoot into the sky
With people inside like prisoners and don't come down for years
It's funny, what's up there . . . in space.

Charlie Smith (11)
St Bede's Catholic High School, Lytham

My Family

I love my family
They care for me
I will start with the youngest.

First, there is Elise
She is so cute.
Then it's Katie
She is as quiet as a mouse.
But then it is Emma
She is as loud as a lion.

Then it's Courtney
She is a drama queen.
And then it is Judie,
She is an amazing singer.
Then it is my mum,
She can be so kind.

Then it's my dad,
He is so funny.
And then it's Matthew.
Now he can cook.
My family may sound complicated
But that's why I love them so much.

Andrew Lonican (12)
St Bede's Catholic High School, Lytham

Where Is The Love?

Fires blazing everywhere,
Buildings set alight,
There is terror in the air,
You don't know who to trust.

People running, people screaming,
People pleading, people weeping,
People falling, people bleeding,
People crying, people dying.

Bangs of guns fill the air,
Cries of children meet them there,
Flashes of light, flames turn red,
There is havoc all around.

People shooting, people killing,
People bombing, people marching,
People fighting, people brawling,
People shouting, people crawling.

Dark is falling once again,
War will still continue,
Raging through the ruined town,
The enemy won't give up.

Emily McIndoe (12)
St Bede's Catholic High School, Lytham

Maisey-Moo

I opened the box
And there she was
As cute and cuddly
As could be.
With big brown eyes
Like chocolate drops
She ran away
So we had to call the cops.
I went on holiday
Having fun, turning red
Until I found out
My poor doggie was dead.
Now I stand and wait in sadness
Wishing she was still here
But I know it will never happen
So we will have to wait till next year.

Gabriella Mulhall (12)
St Bede's Catholic High School, Lytham

Football

The legends of the past
Cantona, Pelé and Best.
We've better players nowadays
With Kaká and the rest.

The nets are shaking
And we keep waiting
For a goal, goal.

The fans are screaming
And the Stretford End is roaring.
It won't be long
Till Ronaldo is scoring.

The nets are shaking
And we keep waiting
For a goal, goal.

Alex Cowalsky (11)
St Bede's Catholic High School, Lytham

Music Of The Ages

From Beethoven and Bach,
To Black Sabbath and Queen,
From smooth and calm,
Into mild and crazy,
The smoothness of Mozart,
The wildness of Angus Young,
From opera and concert halls,
To stadiums and fields,
From the coldness of Kraftwerk,
To the sarcasm of The Sex Pistols,
From Leopold's 'Minuet',
To Iron Maiden's 'The Trooper',
From Beethoven's 'Ecossaise',
To Guns 'n' Roses 'Welcome to the Jungle',
From Franz Schubert's 'Ländler',
To The Clash's 'London Calling'.

James Barnett
St Bede's Catholic High School, Lytham

Dance

We don't stop dancing when we grow old
We grow old when we stop dancing.
A couple that looks exactly like you and me
Dancing in the mirror in perfect harmony
Your gentle, yet protective hand upon my waist
We turn toward each other and I see your face
The frozen smile is growing heavy around this place
As a lively swing tune picks up the pace.
Tears of happiness and joy start to well up in my eyes
And my smile shines so brightly, I could light up the skies.

Shannon O'Hagan (13)
St Bede's Catholic High School, Lytham

Fashion Frenzy

Models on the catwalk,
Spectators admiring the view,
The new spring trends
Designed for me and you.

Paris, Milan, London or New York,
The new trends are everyone's talk.
Spotty stripy, pink or green,
The new designs are now to be seen.

Kate Moss, Lily Cole and Naomi Campbell,
Size zero trends are such a bore.
But people say,
'We want more!'

Eyeliner, foundation, mascara and more
These shoes make my feet sore!
High heels, tiny skirts
Spectators stare in a daze
For spring's new fashion craze.

Millie Gallagher (12)
St Bede's Catholic High School, Lytham

Recycle, Recycle

Recycle, recycle, don't throw away,
your rubbish could help to make a car someday,
tins and plastic could help to make a basket,
and your cardboard could help to make a dartboard,
your paper and plastic could maybe be elastic,
so recycle, recycle, don't throw away
'cause your rubbish could help to make anything someday!

Alan Adams (12)
St Bede's Catholic High School, Lytham

Fashion

Looking through the windows so bright
Seeing the clothes shining with light
Jeans and a top look so well
Oh, as it rang a bell
Already got 'cause I've got fashion
Pastel colours in autumn
Dark colours in winter
My wardrobe has bright red to dark black
Walking down the High Street
Nipping into New Look and Primark
Getting plenty of clothes I like
Oh I got passion for fashion
Silky black trousers with a shirt and waistcoat
As I wore on my thirteenth birthday
I invited all my friends but
I stood out with my waistcoat
Oh so bright
Fashion not just clothes
Its shoes as well
I have a wardrobe of shoes
Like as big as a house
I love going into Faith
As it has the best shoes in the world
It may be expensive but they're cute and cool
Clothes and shoes can be
Spotty dots, squares and stripes
Oh well, that's fashion.

Rebecca Griffiths (12)
St Bede's Catholic High School, Lytham

Terrorism

I remember when I was a boy,
at the age of eight,
I was living in Saudi Arabia,
and then a massive tragedy happened.
That night there was an explosion,
a big one.
Terrorists had shot compound guards
and blown up part of the compound.
And one part was my school,
killing 40 people.
This struck me.
These people, terrorists aren't thinking right.
Most of them are fundamentalists.
This can be very dangerous,
they won't let anyone in their way,
this can become serious.
These people want power,
and want to rule.
They have weapons,
ready to kill,
knives, guns and even bombs!
These people will go to great lengths,
as far as blowing themselves up,
just to kill people.
Some people will have sadness in their lives,
they will have nowhere to go.
They might be brainwashed,
or even forced to do this instead,
they could also be on drugs
and drugs can destroy your life.
There are lots of deaths and cruelty
with these people.
These people are like tigers, are hungry as ever.
I have been one of those who has seen sadness!

Oliver Dent (11)
St Bede's Catholic High School, Lytham

Sports Mad

I love sports
The energy of athletics
The speed of football players
The muscles in weightlifters
It's unbelievable.

So there I am
Drinking my water
Thinking of what I could become.
The warm up is almost over
It is now time
The first race of the Olympics 2012.

The wind's strength is picking up magnificently
Almost lifting me off the ground.

Bang! The gun fires out its bullet,
I am sprinting towards the finish line.
I have tripped over somebody's else's leg
The player has fouled me inside the penalty box.
I am stepping up to take it
I place the ball onto the cone,
'Hooray!' roars the crowd.
It goes through the two poles,
He is out!
That was a tremendous bowl by the Australian
The next batsman is in,
He is looking to hit a drive,
That was a wonderful drive,
In fact it is a hole in one!

I love all sorts of sports,
I especially enjoy the ones on the tennis courts.
You may sweat but that is the way it will go if you want to win a bet.

Danny Scarlett (12)
St Bede's Catholic High School, Lytham

War

War is terrible
Like a weed.
Starts with an argument
Begins with a seed.
Continues with a fight
Carries on with a stem.
Affects next door countries
They join in.
Destroys the next door plant
And then it is a weed
Advances with warfare
All means of death used.
The gardener gets the weed killer,
The war just gets stronger,
The gardener gives up, the weed is too strong.
The world is destroyed
The garden is just a hidden battlefield of dead plants.

Ciaran Dearnley (12)
St Bede's Catholic High School, Lytham

The Generation Of . . .

I have changed a lot over many years
Years ago I was black and white like a zebra
And now I am as colourful as a rainbow

You can find out lots of information from me
You can watch me at any time of the day or night
You can watch all types of things from me
Like soaps, concert, competitions, documentaries,
The news and lots more

I was quite fat and small at first
And now I am wide and thin
Everyone has at least one of me.

What am I?

Rachael Wilson
St Bede's Catholic High School, Lytham

A Golden Beach

Sometimes I sit by my window at night,
Wondering if this should be my life,

I'm a bit different you see, a lot more tanned than most,
I wonder if I should live on the coast?

Of a golden beach, hot sunny days,
Lying on a sun bed catching the rays,

Playing football in nothing but just my bare feet,
Running in the sand of a golden beach,

I know I'm England through and through,
But when I go abroad I fit in too,

When I shop on holiday they speak their language,
But I reply sorry I'm English not Spanish,

There must be foreign in me somewhere down the line,
But I haven't a clue which country is mine,

I'm not against my country, I love it to bits,
But sometimes I sit down and start to think.

Jack Errington (14)
St Bede's Catholic High School, Lytham

Planes

Flying and soaring through the air
Seeing all the views
With these tiny oval eyes.
I see colours of the rainbow
With these eyes of mine,
Colours like
Yellow, orange, red and blue
All beautiful colours of the sky.
I am a metallic metal bird
Soaring up in the air.

Jennifer Hodson (12)
St Bede's Catholic High School, Lytham

How Punishment Has Changed: Through A Child's Eyes

She whipped me and beat me,
She gave me detention,
She held me at gunpoint,
She put me in a corner with a dunces hat on.
She nearly killed me,
With the guillotine and rope noose.
I begged and I pleaded,
I tried to escape,
But she wouldn't put an end to this torture.
Why was she doing this?
This awful thing?
I closed my eyes
And it was all a dream,
A nightmare - something not true.
I really hoped so,
As there was nothing I could do.
I opened my eyes,
She was still there,
I was stranded and helpless: just standing there.
Why did this happen?
Why was I there?
The reason this happened was . . .
I said I didn't care.

Catherine Aitken
St Bede's Catholic High School, Lytham

Celebrity Meltdown

Drugs, sex, rock and roll
Watch out or you'll lose your soul.
Paris Hilton seeks her fame
But we all know she's playing a game.
Britney Spears finds it hard to cope
To calm down she smokes a load of dope.
She finds it really hard to chill
She's got a doctor that gives her a pill.
Amy Winehouse drinks by the litre
Her husband is a real wife beater.
Barbie, she is really plastic
You could break her with a piece of elastic.
Elvis Presley was the king
Especially when he came to sing.
Jade Goody lost her fame
Because she turned and played the wrong game.
Bob Marley was the king of speed
He died shortly after from smoking too much weed.
I got my beauty from my mother
I don't want any other.
So come on boys, let's get it on
Because you all know I'm number one.

Dominique Nuttall (14)
St Bede's Catholic High School, Lytham

A Planet Mourning

Coughing and spluttering through the toxic fumes
Nearly fainting from the heat
The polar caps melting, too quick; too soon
Though scientists won't admit defeat
I'm a planet mourning
The sun cooks the land to a thousand degrees
It has brought me unwillingly to my knees
Plants, trees all set alight
No chance of saving them, try as I might
The Apocalypse is dawning.
Lava flowing like blood from a wound
They're starting to realise their mission is doomed
Cracks rip open my tender skin
Earthquakes swallow up my fellow kin
I'm sweating through to the end.
Why did I go it, I wonder why?
They bore into my flesh
Removing chunks of the land, collapsing the world
I'm sinking into oblivion.
Devastated I lay down to die
The oceans crashing down, cleaning my scars
The humans I blame for killing me and my people
Justice strikes back, it's judgement time
And I'm a planet mourning.
It is slowly crushing my feeble resistance
The bombs are dropping, war is rising
I scream out in agony
The oil and waste dropped in my waters
Shall now be swept away.
Rage and fury blind my hindsight
They have done enough
The crack of lightning, the roar of thunder
It's my turn in this fight.
I tried to warn them, I really did
To stop and save what's left
But did they listen? Did they hell
Who survives? I will not tell.
Not everyone deserves to die
Think it as I may, I know it's a lie

But the damage is done, a stalemate
They're gone forever, the slate wiped clean
I can only remember them in my dreams
Oh what have I done? I repent, I repent
I'm truly a planet mourning.

John Beattie (14)
St Bede's Catholic High School, Lytham

Picture Changes Throughout The Ages

The picture is in black and white
It looks like it's taken in the night
The people are wearing funny clothes
Times were hard then and it shows

The cameras were big and bold
Even the newest ones looked old
They were heavy, some had stands
They weren't made for dainty hands

When coloured photographs came to be
It was great to be able to see
Each person dressed in colours bright
No longer did it appear to be night

Slowly the cameras became smaller
The people on the pictures seemed to grow taller
Camera features changed through the ages
The best ones cost you all your wages

Today there are so many and the prices vary
Some need a degree to understand them so be very wary
They have changed so much throughout the years
Learning how they work may reduce you to tears.

Scott Richardson (11)
St Bede's Catholic High School, Lytham

War

I can hear sirens blurring in my head
I'm led in my bed.
My windows blackened out,
Wondering what's happening behind them.
Lights are flashing.
A bomb could fall any second
And wipe out the whole of London.
I'm shivering with fear.
My mum comes running into my room
Shouting for me to run to the air raid shelter.
My window shatters just as I'm out of my room.
I slip on my slippers
And run quickly out of the house.
A bomb has exploded not so far away.
My grandma's house is no longer there.
The air raid sirens go off again.
I don't quite make it to the air raid shelter
Before another bomb goes off, closer this time.
The lights and fire make my face glow.
My heart starts beating.
Faster and faster.
I can't find my mum!
I start panicking. Where is she?
I can feel tears rolling down my cheeks.
My mum is led on the floor about 10 metres away
Blood streaming down her face.
Bits of her body blown off and scattered around her.
I try to run to the air raid shelter once again
But a bomb had wiped that out too.
All that was left was my mum's heart locket.

Rebecca Salthouse (11)
St Bede's Catholic High School, Lytham

A Brand New Piece Of Technology

Look at me, a brand new piece of technology,
All shiny and ready for using,
A box like a TV,
All metallic and ready as ever,
I have a monitor all bright with loads of information,
To do things on my monitor I have a mouse,
A little metallic clicky mouse,
Along with a keyboard of many keys to do lots of typing
(not homework!),
To get the document onto paper I have a printer,
It sometimes plays up but on the whole it is a good printer,
That's me, a brand new piece of technology,
Waiting . . . waiting . . .
Waiting for someone to come and use me,
To get out into the stores and be sold as fast as I can,
For them to look at me,
A brand new piece of technology.

Antonia Hunter (11)
St Bede's Catholic High School, Lytham

Lights

Lights amuse me, there are lots of different types,
There's big and small, even some on bikes.
There's lots of different colours, blue, green and red,
There's some on the wall to help you sleep in bed.
Some don't look like it but are in the shape of a pear,
There are lots of different shapes, like a rectangle or a square.
Some are very lucky and could help light up the Queen,
Others not so lucky and light up a sloppy teen.
You can have whatever types of lights you like
As long as you think about it,
It could be waterproof, windproof, purple and green
Stuck on your PE kit.

Alice Fletcher (11)
St Bede's Catholic High School, Lytham

Ocean

Rolling surf amongst the waves
Foiling surfers, in others gaze
In their attempt for glory and praise

This is an ocean

The coral cities beneath the waves
Colours of the rainbow
Colours to gaze

This is an ocean

The scaly fish
Refuse to wish
Of land beyond this glistening sea

This is an ocean

No nets amongst
This glistening sea
Free for the fish, free for me

But this is not the ocean that I see

I see a green sea
No people, no fish, nothing to see
But long pipes, spewing thick green sludge

That once in, will never budge

And they call this an ocean

No fish to see
They died years ago
Nothing but the carcasses left to see
In this barren wasteland

And they call this an ocean

Only scavengers search this sea
For the small amounts of food, that they can see
Amongst this green, barren wasteland

And they call this an ocean

No surfers to see
Cruising the thick, green waves
In their place rubbish and trash

And they call this an ocean.

Kyle Daniels (14)
St Bede's Catholic High School, Lytham

I'm A Nuclear Bomb

I'm a nuclear bomb,
Don't worry I'm nice,
All my brothers and sisters are evil,
I'm scared for me and you,
I don't want to kill myself or you,
You try to stop us,
But nothing works,
I'm being blown up in 5 minutes,
I'm right next to the London Eye,
Bye and please forgive me.

Silence,
Then suddenly *bang, bang!* It's started,
You run, hearing deathly screams on the way,
You think once you're in a shelter you're safe
But *bang, bang!* And you're not,
The scene all around you, bloody red,
Deadly orange and the slight
Blackness of the sky,
Then when you think it'll never end, *boom, boom!*
Silence, but this time it's deadly.

Helen Elsender-Harris (11)
St Bede's Catholic High School, Lytham

Tigers

With their diamond eyes,
Like spy goggles,
They see for miles,
With their fierce smiles,
They can look like a log,
But leap out of the misty fog,
Black as night stripes,
Like orange and black knights,
They stalk you like eagles flying,
You don't know where they could be lying.
Leaping nearer and nearer,
Coming to get you,
Gobble you up,
It's here, don't shoot,
It just wants some meat.
Don't shoot . . .
Bang!

Simon Dewhurst (11)
St Bede's Catholic High School, Lytham

Cats

Small, tall, thin and fat,
They've all been said about a cat.
Sly slithers here and there,
Upstairs, downstairs, everywhere.
Piercing eyes when catching prey,
Their main aim throughout the day.
Tucked up warm and cosy at night
Fearless opponents, a vicious fight.
Stalking people down the street,
In and out the clumsy feet.
Blended colours within the fur,
A pesky hiss, a cute loving purr . . .
Small, tall, thin and fat
They've all been said about a cat.

Beth Birch (12)
St Bede's Catholic High School, Lytham

The Revolution Of Fashion

Think right back to World War II,
The clothes they had were very few,
It seemed like nothing to us right now,
But having two T-shirts was a real big wow.

Moving on to the 70s,
Most people think of hippies,
Tie-dyeing T-shirts and flowers in their hair,
Standing up for what wasn't fair.

Then came the 80s,
Fluorescent and dazzling,
Permed hair and colourful,
Leg warmers were wonderful.

In stroll the 90s,
Bronze, silver and gold,
Shell suits and cat suits,
Fashion that grows old.

Entering the new Millennium was such a big thing,
Colours are everywhere, pastels for spring,
Summer is yellow, red and white,
Winter is blue and not so bright.

Now we're in autumn there's lots to be seen,
Everyone in brown and also green,
All the shades of purple are absolutely in,
Everything else just goes in the bin.

Fashion, fashion, fashion,
Sent from in the heavens,
Changing, changing all the time,
Who knows what's next in line?

Gina Godsiff (11)
St Bede's Catholic High School, Lytham

War

Bang!
The heavy guns fire.
My friends fall beside me,
Casualties piling up.

Bullets sound,
Friends turn into corpses.
The enemy,
As vicious as animals.

The countdown starts,
Danger lurks round every corner.
Blood flowing like a wild river,
The rotten stench hangs around the area.

War is a miserable place,
Hope seems a long distance from me.
I fight on,
Hoping to be lucky.

Bang!
That one sound.
As a gun fires,
And I fall to the ground.

On the stretcher,
Pain building up.
No more war for me,
For I am happy with what I've done,
And what I've become.

David McConachie (13)
St Bede's Catholic High School, Lytham

Are We Home Yet?

In peace sons bury their fathers,
In war fathers bury their sons,
Cruel hatred plagues the air,
Bloodshed all around me,
People dying,
When will it be me?

Time does not fly here,
It crawls,
Stopping at every living thing to snarl or hiss,
My time will never end here for memories are not forgotten,
My hollow heart pumps in dire need of repair,
Invisible stones dragging,
When will I be free?

Food is scarce,
Water is rare,
Ammunition is used,
Everyone is accused,
Bullets flaring,
Shells dropping,
Grenades exploding,
Blood spilling,
When will it be mine?

When will I come home,
Will it ever be known?
Over here time is unknown.

Craig McCann (11)
St Bede's Catholic High School, Lytham

A Scarlet Bird

I fly across the sky bold and brave,
Like a scarlet bird, skimming the bed of clouds.

My wings get hotter, turning metallic-red,
When they see the burning ball of flames.

In my belly are the passengers in a sleepy, dreamy mood,
Peeping out through the oval windows.

The pilot takes control of me,
As he looks out through my clear blue eyes.

Below me now is the watery blue sea,
Shimmering like glitter, moving in slow motion.

The pilot says to the passengers, 'Seatbelts allowed off.'
I hear them all sigh and relax.

I feel the pilot twist me and turn me,
As he tries to land me on the ground.

Then finally he lands me and all the passengers unload,
And there I stay, waiting for the next flight.

Emily Shea (11)
St Bede's Catholic High School, Lytham

Poverty

Tiny, lifeless bodies, in sad, caring arms.
Illegal money being made on cocoa farms.
Just born babies, as thin as a stick.
Children with Kalashnikovs, blood running thick.

Whole families living off one piece of bread.
Drinking dirty water, soon they'll be dead.
Wearing the same clothes, year after year.
Adolescent militia is the least of their fear.

No technology, hygiene, only happiness in Heaven.
God as my witness, I pray for them.

Guy Hay (14)
St Bede's Catholic High School, Lytham

Generation Rap

This is my life
This is how it goes
Tell you all a little story
I just want you to know
I've been so foolish, so afraid
To cover all this, hurt and pain
So check my style and check my flow
No doubt about it, I'll end up with five oh
On my last warning with the police
You can't really get rid of me
Am strong in the arms
But messed in the head
All you other girls better drop dead
I've felt so much pain
Am going insane
Why won't it just go away?
Feels like a rush on ecstasy
Just lets take control of me
Just go with the flow and don't hold back
I'll give you MC's a lesson not to forget
Step up to me, it'll be real hard
'Cause you're just a piece of lard
This is my life
Might seem a mess
But you other girls
Just sit back
Try and look your best.

Abi Donovan (14)
St Bede's Catholic High School, Lytham

Love Is A Different Thing

I'm now a handsome young lad,
It's now the end of school,
This poem is about me and how I made myself a fool.

I'm ready to show my cool side,
I'm looking for a girl for me,
I have to be as calm as possible and as cool as I can be.

The thing about girls is this,
They are very hard to get,
You can't buy them, or swap them, not if you place a bet.

The best place to get girls is a pub,
Where the most beautiful girls crash,
I decided to show off, juggle some bottles
But I dropped them and they went *smash!*

I ran to the café to hide,
I walked up to the table when *bump!*
A beautiful young girl, who seemed very upset,
She explained everything, she was dumped!

I cheered her up soon enough,
I did my very best,
I asked if we could go out,
And what do you know? She said yes!

So there we were, talking to each other,
We were in love like no other,
She said I was a handsome prince,
I said she was as pretty as Cleopatra.

So this I learnt, a single lesson,
The love and care I bring,
But remember this when you want a girl,

Love is a different thing.

Frazer Gillgrass (12)
St Bede's Catholic High School, Lytham

Mobile Phones

Look at me, look at me
I am a mobile phone.
I am shiny and blue and as skinny as a model.
Look at me, look at me
I am a mobile phone.

Look at me, look at me
I am a mobile phone.
Nowadays it's a bit like a competition
Between phones and who's old and new
Who's cool and who's not.
Look at me, look at me
I am a mobile phone.

Look at me, look at me
I am a mobile phone.
Isn't it amazing how a small thing
Like this can do so many things.
Look at me, look at me
I am a mobile phone.

Look at me, look at me
I am a mobile phone.
She uses me all the time,
She makes me play music in front of her friends
She always pushes my buttons to talk to her friend Carly,
She's always chatting to her.
Look at me, look at me
I am a mobile phone.

Look at me, look at me
I am a mobile phone.
Sometimes I wish I could be something else
Like a plane, because they go all over the place,
All I do is follow boring Meg around all day.
Look at me, look at me
I am a mobile phone.

Meg Simi (12)
St Bede's Catholic High School, Lytham

Fashion Expresses Me, What About You?

It always seems to find its way back into the shop windows,
Leggings, shoes, handbags and hair.
What goes around comes around,
But how and where?

I am confused about most things,
Multiplying, dividing, spelling and basically that's who I am.
But fashion isn't one of these things,
When it comes to fashion, I'm not a lamb.

I don't really follow everyone else,
But who says that's what I have to do.
Sometimes I'm not good at designing the best outfits,
But I bet you're not too.

I like fashion because it's full of colour.
It's like a firework,
If you wear a crazy colour,
People won't stare or smirk.

Fashion is like people,
Some you like, some you don't.
Some things may look the same, but that's definitely not true.
Look a little deeper into the cotton next time
and you might find you.

Next time you go shopping,
You look for me and I'll look for you.
I'll be the outrageous one,
But will you be too?

Tess Healey (12)
St Bede's Catholic High School, Lytham

Animal Cruelty

Animals, animals all around.

Cute, beautiful and furry
they make you happy when you kiss them and cuddle them.
Big cats, little dogs, big dogs, little cats,
all kinds of different types.

But in different parts of the world
there is blood and gore everywhere,
little puppies stuck down holes
and little kittens run over by cars.

Beautiful lions and tigers killed for their fur.
Elephants killed for tusks.

Tigers, monkeys, lions and more
all brought into captivity and locked behind bars.

Animals, animals all around,
we have to try and help them.

Louise Taylor (12)
St Bede's Catholic High School, Lytham

Skiing

The cold crisp snow crunches underneath you
as you gently glide down the slope.
You get to the bottom with a grin on your face
and think, what fun and do it again.
Going to the top you look down
and people beneath you look like little dots.
You've reached the very top and get ready to go,
1, 2, 3 and off you go.
Going down so very fast.
Side to side you go, speeding down,
shoop, shoop, shoop.
You reach the bottom
and your cheeks are as red as a rose.
You feel so very ready to go do it again.

Robyn Turcsanyi (11)
St Bede's Catholic High School, Lytham

In The Past

The green grass sparkles in the sun,
Some fans shouting, 'Go on my son!'
The boots are green, the boots are yellow,
I really feel sorry for that young fellow.
Standing out from all the rest,
With them plastic boots he can't be the best.
Heading a ball that's like a brick,
Heading a ball that's like a feather.
Prancing around with lots of joy,
Which ball they head they have no choice.
Diving round like a fish out of water
Broken legs, but they carry on.
Playing with the 8-1-1
Up against the 4-4-2.
The groundsman closes up for the night,
When he comes back tomorrow he'll have a fright.

Sean Hogarth (14)
St Bede's Catholic High School, Lytham

My Generation As A Chav . . .

Blue lights flashing
Police cars crashing

Had a hard life running
Had to be very cunning

My friends know I am wagging
My energy is sagging

My life is hell
The police put me in a cell

No way of getting out
All I want to do is scream and shout

Didn't mean to kill my friend
I wish my life would just come to an end . . .

Reece Campbell (14)
St Bede's Catholic High School, Lytham

Football In This Generation

Arriving in their flash new cars,
And brand new shining suits.
Cameras flashing all around them.
Could life get any better
In this generation?

They change into their gleaming white kit,
Then slip on their slick new boots,
Made specially for their talents.
In this generation, everything seems perfect.

Tens of thousands of fans chant their name
As they stroll out onto a perfectly cut pitch,
For another weekly game.

When the game is over,
A quick change and then back home
To a house like you have never seen before,
The drive's piled up with brand new cars
And even a polished door.

Butlers and maids help them for ages
Paid for with their tremendous wages.
Thirty to one hundred thousand pounds a week
Not bad for a job that seems so easy.

So much has changed over the years,
Ups and downs, smiles and cheers.
It seems so good and not too bad
To be a footballer
In this generation.

David Newhouse (13)
St Bede's Catholic High School, Lytham

Fashion/Money

Fashion

Fashion, fashion is a great passion,
Bright and bold,
Colourful gold.

Fashion, fashion is a great passion,
Living colours all around me,
So colourful I can't see.

Fashion, fashion is a great passion,
Hats, hats,
Made out of cats,
Big and small, give me a call.

Fashion, fashion is a great passion,
High heel shoes,
Never loose,
Fashion, fashion is a great passion.

Money

Money is great,
Money is fine,
I wish it could be all mine,
All to spend,
All to give,
What a great life to live,
Spend it on clothes,
Spend it on food.

Money is great,
Money is fine,
I spend most of it on wine,
Spend it on charities,
Or on a bag of peas,
But money is great,
Money is fine,
One day,
It's all mine.

Francine Hewson (11)
St Bede's Catholic High School, Lytham

What Am I?

I go in the night,
I go in the day,
Never give up, that's what I say.
What am I?

Images pass like a cheetah,
Buildings and mountains, that's what I see,
Over bridges and bumps too . . .
I must not give up!
What am I?

Stars appear and disappear,
Through Lime Street and Euston I change gear,
I've travelled the world, through many ages.
What am I?

My appearance is unattractive,
But I'm strong inside.
I carry people old and new,
Chugga-chug-chug, chugga-chug-chug.
What am I?

Kyle Butler (11)
St Bede's Catholic High School, Lytham

Real Like Real

As I switched on,
I knew it was done.
The lights started flashing,
I knew I would have won.
The race was near to the finish,
I knew it was for fun.
Now that it was over,
I know my friend had gone.

Josh Bilsborough (13)
St Bede's Catholic High School, Lytham

Gallop Of Hooves

Galloping across the beach,
wind in my hair,
blue sky.
Chopping sea, people watching,
home.
Competition time,
judges watching, crowds cheering,
off we go, over the first jump,
through the water,
trophies to win,
rosettes to hold.
She's my friend and companion,
I brush her soft, clean coat,
I give her a mint,
I stroke her nose softly,
she is my horse
and I am proud of her.
I put her in the field, with her friends,
she rolls on the cold grass,
she loves the freedom.
I bring her in at night,
I give her the food,
she lays in the warm straw,
I turn the light off, she sleeps.
I tack her up ready for another hack.
We gallop the fields,
she runs so fast,
I love the excitement and the thrill.

Charlotte Newsham (13)
St Bede's Catholic High School, Lytham

Computers

A vast window of information
In which anything can be seen
You can find out everything
From that electronic screen

A place of free speech, which can be heard
From anyone around the world
Chatrooms and forums and MSN
Free to use again and again

The screen is full of plasma
The pixels creating images
Creating the full spectra
Millions and millions of choices

There's amazing software you can get
You can zoom in on your house
The computer's a brilliant asset
All you need is a monitor, keyboard and a mouse

But it's also a terrible thing
Free speech isn't always good
There's stuff like internet bullying
Ruining people's childhoods

But there's always more good than bad
So I think we still should use it
It's a privilege and I will never abuse it.

Joe Incorvaya (14)
St Bede's Catholic High School, Lytham

Guitar

I pick up the guitar of a brilliant blue
The one for me, I always knew
Its body hard, its texture soft
A worthy model of a worthy cost

Its neck points straight up to the sky
I'm feeling happy, I'm feeling high
I pluck the strings, it feels so good
It sounds so warm, just like it should

I'm playing fast, I'm playing loud
Not for the money, but for the crowd
Heads start to bang and people cheer
The brutality pierces every ear

As I finish with a final bang
One last chord and a cymbal clangs
A final cheer and bid farewell
The guitar will be back, only time will tell!

Mike Severyn (13)
St Bede's Catholic High School, Lytham

The Hoodie And I

As I walked down the side of Hoodie Lane
This old guy shot me a look of shame.
I thought that he could just stuff off
When this other young hoodlum said, 'Hey, nice cloth!'
I thought right, now I have reached the end of my tether
And the fact that I'm stood in this f-f-f-freezing weather.
That's it, I'm off to the shops to get some new clothes
And I am gonna set these things alight on the flaming stone.
I really don't like these people who talk behind my back
So they'd best get back before I *attack!*

Joseph Harrison (13)
St Bede's Catholic High School, Lytham

My Generation

Being a teenager is not that much fun.
Druggies and violence, the shrieks of a gun.
Fag ends and bottles smashed on the floor.
Being a teenager is such a bore.

Teenagers swearing and wearing their hoods.
People vandalising other's goods.
Mugging and thieving
Just to impress a girl.

Listening to that 'chavy' dance music all the time.
Getting so bored they commit a crime.
Nike, Adidas, Timberland and Lacoste, what's the reason?
The violence goes on from season to season.

So all those chavs think they're hard and cool
But really they're acting like fools.
They need to stop their chavy ways
And be respectful for the rest of their days.

Kitty Ward-Smith (12)
St Bede's Catholic High School, Lytham

Tall Paul

There once was a man called Paul,
Who boasted that he was so tall,
But one day something occurred,
And now he is very small.
He got laughed at,
For being small,
And he shouted, 'I want to be tall!'
So God said,
'You can be tall again if you never boast again.'
He said he wouldn't
So God made him tall,
He grew tall and never boasted again.

Matthew James (13)
St Bede's Catholic High School, Lytham

Blown Away

Living to see the next May Day
Before the world is blown away
Thinking, *why am I here*
With my family I hold so dear?
Other children are not so cherished
They have seen their parents perished
In a hole six feet under.
In a box, it makes you wonder
Why the world is a place
Children seen with a sad face.
It makes me wonder why on the day
All the buses got blown away.
That's why the world is so sad
Because the terrorists are really bad.
We should not be the ones suffering pain
When at times the world seems insane
Feelings and innocence cast asunder
Please let's have a world filled with peace and wonder.

Adam Tranter (15)
St Bede's Catholic High School, Lytham

I Want Answers

I feel angry
I feel sad
You really were the worst dad.

You were meant to care
You were always meant to be there.

But you left
In the night
Giving us all such a fright.

I want answers
Why and where?
But this hate for you will always be there.

Emma Kelly (14)
St Bede's Catholic High School, Lytham

Mobiles

Mobiles, mobiles,
Here, now, then they are gone,
Ring and a ding, a buzz and a beeb beeb.

Mobiles, mobiles,

My mobile is my second heart,
I can't survive without it,
They take pictures and calls.

Mobiles, mobiles,

My mobile is like a disco,
Every three seconds, *flash, flash, flash,*
Flashing blue, purple and red,
Music playing.

Mobiles, mobiles,

Wallpapers, screensavers,
Internet and bluetooth,
Mobiles, mobiles, mobiles.

Ash-Leigh Murphy (11)
St Bede's Catholic High School, Lytham

Rage!

His hands clenched with rage
he became too dangerous to touch,
blinded by the rage in his eyes
he was a human killing machine.

He elevated his arm
like he was about to shoot,
invincible was his name,
hurt and harm was his game.

Once again he struck
to the love of his life,
one hit can do a lot,
especially with a knife.

Sarah Ingham (13)
St Bede's Catholic High School, Lytham

The Tragic Story Of War

If it wasn't for war I wouldn't be in this state.
It all began in October,
the night air was cold and breezy.
Machine gun bullets were scraping my helmet,
and grenades were exploding near me.
Not even the bunker could save me now.
'Incoming rocket at 50mph!' said the voiceover from Command.
'Over and out!' I placed my radio back in my pocket.

I was a believer in history, and I joined the war in Iraq,
for Queen and Country.
I said to myself, *I either stay here and die*
or leave my post and fight on the battlefield.
'Incoming missile in 5, 4, 3!' said the voiceover.
At that moment I jumped out of the bunker,
rolled 5 metres on the ground
and my vision faded.

The next time I opened my eyes,
I was sitting in a bed.
The blurriness in my eyes had faded,
there was a lady in white.
'Where am I?' I asked her.
'You are in a hospital wing,
the rocket exploded when you were unconscious,
and your foot was blown off,' said the nurse.
'Luckily a fellow soldier,
pulled your body away from more damage,'
she told me.
I looked down at my cast and screamed,
the pain came to me like it had never been there.

Luckily I'm still here today, telling you the story.
War is a bad thing, it changed my view about history.
I'm not as loyal to Queen and Country as I used to be,
the person I'm most loyal to now is God,
the one that stopped me from death.

Luke Williams (11)
St Bede's Catholic High School, Lytham

What Am I?

I can be large or small,
It depends when you bought me.
But I've always been the same colour.
What am I?

I'm either black or metallic,
Never light, always dark.
I turn hot when I am on.
What am I?

Like a snake,
My wire slithers across the hard floor.
My mouth goes into the wall.
What am I?

I can be rather expensive,
It depends when you bought me.
I've been around quite a long time now.
What am I?

The part that heats up is my mouth,
My mouth is the part that makes no curls.
Though it burns you if you get angry.
What am I?

There are many types of me,
But I'm a GHD!
I can be bought online or instore.
What am I?

I've told you all you need to know,
So now look at the clues.
I'm a GHD!

What am I?
Hair straighteners.

Emily Duxbury (11)
St Bede's Catholic High School, Lytham

Weapons Of War

Bang!
The machine guns fire
Bang!
The handguns fire
With a flurry of bullets

Booming sounds,
Rotting corpses
And deaths,
With a lot of pain

People shouting
Guns firing
Danger everywhere
Puddles of blood wherever you step

Shiny black metal
Heavy artillery
Light artillery
Pain around every corner

It was like a war
Against two armies
But also crime
Murderers everywhere

I am scared but also happy
I know it will end
Sometime now, there it was
Like a flash I was dead.

Luke Jones (14)
St Bede's Catholic High School, Lytham

Food

Food is great,
It keeps us alive,
Never dies,
It helps you survive,
All colours are different,
You can have lots,
Red, yellow, orange, green,
Purple, pink, blue, cream,
When you eat some it makes you cringe
And others make you sick,
Some foods you enjoy,
Some foods you hate,
Sometimes you are hungry
And just have to wait,
Other times you are thirsty
And just get a drink,
We all need to eat,
And oh such a treat,
Potatoes and carrots
And succulent meat,
We think of the crops grown in the field
With the sunshine and rain
They'll give a good yield,
When they go into the shops,
We can buy the great big crops.

Joanna Little (11)
St Bede's Catholic High School, Lytham

Football

The crisp green grass lit up by the golden sunlight,
The net gently blowing in a soft cool breeze,
The roar of the crowd illuminates the ground,
Two teams of eleven walk out side by side,
Kaká, Messi, Ronaldinho and Cannavaro ready to light up the game,
When they walk out of the tunnel,
The sun brightly lights up the ground filled,
The roaring crowd stands with excitement,
Then it begins,
Running this way and that,
Turning here and there,
The bar sharply shakes as the ball bounces off it,
Everyone is on the edge of their seats,
Then with 10 minutes left the first goal goes in,
One side of the ground is in silence,
While one side cheers with relief,
Then the high-pitched whistle of the referee goes off,
One side of the ground cannot believe what they have seen,
As they leave the ground leaving litter behind,
The ground becomes silent like nothing has happened.

Matthew Salisbury (14)
St Bede's Catholic High School, Lytham

Cameras

I carried my long fragile equipment in its large black case.
I set it out,
Through its eye it sees a family.
They pose and smile.
I capture it in a flash.

Their happiness framed on the wall.
Comments pass that moment every day.
Feeling that pleasure whenever,
Is what makes it special.

Freezing memories and moments,
Shapes and lines coloured in,
It's life,
It's evidence.
Treasure everyone.

This wonder only takes a second,
A click,
Then a flash,
Then a picture.

Jess Daniel Nidd (13)
St Bede's Catholic High School, Lytham

Gun Crime

Walking down a dark street,
Scared of the people I could meet.
In their hands was a gun,
They only thought it was a bit of fun.

I walked straight past,
I couldn't bear.
They might have shot someone,
This isn't far.

I checked the news
And there they were.
Laughing and joking,
They just didn't care.

The poor boy's life had just come and gone,
The mum and dad cry on and on.
In their hands was a gun,
They only thought it was a bit of fun.

Becky Sullivan (12)
St Bede's Catholic High School, Lytham

Litter

Litter, litter everywhere
Bugs and slugs here and there
So please put your rubbish in the bins provided
So we can walk the streets with no bugs behind us
Help us to help the environment get fitter
So please find a bin and drop in that litter.

Francesca Galloway (11)
St Bede's Catholic High School, Lytham

My Generation

Guns, knives, hoods and more
Are what most people think
Come with my generation.

Spitting, kicking, swearing and more
Are what most people think
Come with my generation.

Mugging, thieving and running wild
Are what most people think
Come with my generation.

But most of this is not really true
Everything most of us do
Is what you did too.

But some of us are what I have just said
And this is the story of my generation.

Jack Balmer (13)
St Bede's Catholic High School, Lytham

My Generation

Why do adults look down on us,
Just because of our age?
Do they not remember being young once,
Or did they just miss out that stage?

We may listen to iPods,
Or we may have a mobile phone,
But all we want to do is have some fun,
So why do they have to groan?

Why can't they all just relax,
And let us get on with our youth?
We're not all troublemakers,
They don't even have any proof.

Hannah Smith (13)
St Bede's Catholic High School, Lytham

My Daily Troubles

Perfect parents telling what or not to do,
I'm sick of them saying, 'Follow what I do,'
They're embarrassed about who I really am,
And say, 'She's not for you.'

Parents, they should encourage me,
But instead they let me down,
I'm trying so hard to grow up but
They treat me like a child.

Help! I'm so fed up of it,
So help me get along,
Ow! Mum, understand,
It's not me, it's Dan.

I'm working hard in school,
As all around,
My parents don't help me much,
They leave me on my own,
I have a few friends in school,
Not really a rebel,
I help my friends along,
Not too bossy, I think,
These are my daily troubles,
Of my modern life.

Matthew Kondal (12)
St Bede's Catholic High School, Lytham

Blackpool

Blackpool is a great place to stay
So many things to do and to say
So many tourists come every day
And only to say it's the best place to stay.

So many rides and buildings to visit
Like the Big One which stands tall
And the three piers have a great view of the sea
That's why people like them so much.

The beach in Blackpool is very sunny
At night the waves come crashing in
And during the day they make a soothing sound
Once the tide goes out a golden beach is left.

The biggest attraction though is the Tower
For years it has stood there not to be moved
So many people pay a lot every year just to get in
When I went in it was hard to see.

So at the end of this poem there's only one thing to say
That Blackpool is a great place to stay
With all the rides and attractions that make it special
So next time on holiday come to Blackpool.

Elliot Cason (12)
St Bede's Catholic High School, Lytham

The Sea

The blue water crashes against the shore,
The sea has no law,
As it drags out to open water,
When it crashes back onto the shore it sounds like a mortar.

The sea has lots of ships on it every day,
As they go to the bay,
The sea near me is the best,
From above it looks like a bird's nest.

The beach off the sea is as rich as gold,
But is very old,
The golden sand lasts for an age,
But it stands the sea's rage.

The sea near me is the best,
It's better than all the rest,
Soon it may be dead,
Along with the life and its bed.

Curtis Clough (12)
St Bede's Catholic High School, Lytham

My Generation

M ale teenagers wearing hoods. Are they doing any harm?
Y oung bored kids, they just want to have fun.

G uns and violence, should it come down to that.
E very chav wants to fight to impress a girl.
N o to the latest gadgets? Be prepared for bullying!
E very lad and girl wants love with a pretty face,
holding their hand.
R ave on Friday night, including drinking and smoking.
A ll they want to do is party!
T rouble causers! No respect for the elders or environment.
I f my parents find out they just won't understand.
O nly friends understand my problems.
N aughty kids, they're doing it again,
moans the old age citizens.

Sasha Wozniak (12)
St Bede's Catholic High School, Lytham

I Can't Walk Down The Street

I can't walk down the street,
Without being looked at.
The staring eyes that frighten,
Am scared of them, they're scared of me.

I can't walk down the street,
Without being offended.
I have my hood up, they cross the road,
With it down they give dirty looks or murmur.

I can't walk down the street,
Without being stopped.
I try to go in the shop, they watch and turn me away,
The police ask what I'm doing.

I'm doing nothing,
Stop being prejudiced.

Simon Benyon (13)
St Bede's Catholic High School, Lytham

Teens

Being a teenager can be a big stress,
Whether I'm wearing a hoody or even a dress.
People assume I'm going to do wrong,
The glares they give me go on for too long.
Some teenagers always do right,
They work hard from day to night.
But some turn to violence over any little thing,
Getting shot, taking drugs that would defiantly sting!
The pain and suffering. What is the reason?
But this pain will go on from season to season.
Getting punched, getting shot, the trouble never ends
Rather than all this pain why can't they just be friends?
After the pain they have caused they laugh and they joke
They take drugs, they play with guns and they also always smoke.
But some teens don't act quite as bad,
To be treated so badly can be so sad.

Samantha Keeley (12)
St Bede's Catholic High School, Lytham

And Die

The forest doors opened
I entered
The cold scratchy looking branches wove between the trees
All was quiet, all was calm
I stood and waited
Waiting for the long bony hand to reach out and grab my shoulder
The teeth to sink into my neck and suck my blood
For me to fall down on the earthy ground, and die
But nothing happened, nothing at all
I walked on, stopped again and waited
Waiting for the ground to fall from beneath me
The hot lava to pour over my body
For me to fall down on the earthy ground, and die
Still, nothing happened
I didn't see why it was not happening
Again, I walked on
But this time I kept on walking
I did not stop, I kept on walking
I tripped and fell onto the earthy ground, and died.

Chantelle Robinson (12)
St Bede's Catholic High School, Lytham

Monster House

The night before Hallowe'en
All was quiet
Nothing stirred
Apart from the house.

They always said it would awaken
I never believed them
Until I saw it for myself
Odd things were happening, things disappearing.

Then it woke up
It looked as though its eyes were on fire
Then it reared up on its tree-like limbs
And opened its mouth full of rotten teeth
And charged across the street.

When it arrived it stuck its hand in my window
And dragged me out
It was just about to devour me
When I woke up.

Dominic Gray (14)
St Bede's Catholic High School, Lytham

The Day My Life Went Bad

You make me laugh,
You make me smile,
Even just for a little while.

I dream of you,
I see your face.
I open the door,
You're on my case.

The love is gone,
My dream is shattered.
You have left my heart bruised and battered.

I move on,
You drift away.
I live my life from day-to-day.

The happy feeling has all gone,
And so, again, I move on.
This feeling was once so rare.
Now every day I'm in despair.

I hope you're happy,
Now I'm sad
That was the day my life went bad.

Rosie Ward (13)
St Bede's Catholic High School, Lytham

Where Have You Been?

Every day is the same,
day after day,
it all started in reception,
she always gets her way.

My friend Amy who is always late for class,
but when Sir says, 'Where have you been?'
she says she has been with me, Cass.

But I have just been sitting there
with all the other kids.

He says, 'What have you been doing?'
And I say, 'My pop quiz.'

Then he says, 'Is that true?'
and I say, 'Yes it is.'
He says, 'Detention, no more pop quiz.'

I am sitting in detention
not knowing what to do.

Should I be her friend?
What would you do?

Charlotte Naylor (11)
St Bede's Catholic High School, Lytham

Danger

Just because I wear a hoodie,
Doesn't mean I'm trouble,
Maybe it's cold,
Maybe my face is wounded,
But all you think is *danger.*

You may want to cross the road,
Just to avoid my path,
The thing is I am no *danger.*

I try to offer my help,
It's thrown back in my face,
Because I wear a hoodie,
You think that I am *danger.*

Everyone stereotypes me,
Just because of my clothes,
Would you like it?
Trust me, I am no *danger.*

You can't help yourself though,
You need to attack me,
It's not fair!
I am no *danger.*

Everyone thinks I'm a threat,
I could say the same about you,
Then we will see how you like it,
Society should accept me as I am,
Because I am no *danger.*

Vincent Goode (13)
St Bede's Catholic High School, Lytham

My Generation

The problems which we face today,
Never seem to go away,
Arguments, back-stabbing with my friends,
Are ever-lasting, they never end.

Violence, disrespect, graffiti and more,
Tanks, bombs, never-ending war,
Global warming, it's never new,
Being selfish, it's all we do.

Criminals, robbers sent to jail,
I try to help, I always fail,
I have to be what everyone wants,
I never have freedom, not once.

Hoodies? No way! They're not allowed,
But I don't want to join the crowd!
Skinny jeans are emo.
Trackies are chav.
I can have what I want to have.
Smoking, drugs, alcohol, that's rave,
It's all kids do, day by day.

If you don't have a mobile you're not cool,
All this bullying, happens at school.
Adidas, K-Swiss, Etnies and Nike,
This is what my generation's like,
Be who you are, try to go far,
This is who my generation are.

Georgia Leggett (12)
St Bede's Catholic High School, Lytham

Words, Words, Words

Books, poems, posters, homework!
It's all words, words, words.
You see them every day.
At school, at home, even when you play.

But what if they weren't,
They'd been thrown away forever?
Bye, so long, auf wiedersehen, goodbye,
Adieu, adieu, catch ya later, ciao (sigh).

They'd be no more writing,
No need for schools,
Hip hip hooray!
No more words from today!

All the school can be knocked down,
Crushed into tiny pieces,
Bye maths, bye English, bye history,
All the parents would say, 'What a mystery?'

But don't you think you'd get a bit bored?
No one to chat to, or tell secrets to?
I like my words thank you very much,
My words will be forever clutched!

Laura Hall (11)
St Bede's Catholic High School, Lytham

A Good Surprise

Seagulls fly above the bay,
And complete their day,
But one seagull glows like a ruby,
Even horses stop eating their hay.

An amazing discovery may have been found,
As the seagull lands on the ground.
It sheds its wings and blazes in fire,
Still amazing but the day becomes dire.

Snapshots and pictures in the news,
Of a real-life phoenix,
Which flew to many wonders of the Earth,
It then died but was given rebirth!

A national phenomenon had lived for weeks,
But sometimes the system had leaks,
And people faded belief,
Then the phoenix would come back
And give the news some relief.

Michael Reilly (11)
St Bede's Catholic High School, Lytham

Write A Poem About Anything . . . My Mind Goes Blank!

Write a poem about anything
My mind goes blank . . .

Pens, pencils and coloured crayons dance across the page
Fairies, knights and dragons of the medieval age
Unicorns and rainbows
Irish pots of gold
Pens, pencils and coloured crayons dance across the page.

Doors creak, stare into the dark and haunted room
Ghostly ghouls and a zombie corpse chasing after you
Corpse brides and skeleton bones
Just like Hallowe'en
Doors creak, stare into the dark and haunted room.

Flaked fir trees and sparkling lights in the winter breeze
Bright red noses, ready for that long belated sneeze
Jingle of the Christmas bells
Scarves and fleeces too
Flaked fir trees and sparkling lights in the winter breeze.

Write a poem about anything
My mind goes blank.

Francesca Fernandes (13)
St Bede's Catholic High School, Lytham

The Truth

Now I know what I dread,
The truth, it hurts, the painful said,
I wanted to know what was true,
But now I do, I'm not sure I do.

It hurts so bad, night and day,
You have no idea, nothing to say,
Its terrible nature, the horrible truth,
It's destroying me, through and through.

Now I wish I could undo,
What I've done, the pain to you,
It makes me retch, I'm full of remorse,
I'm crying with sadness, it hits me full force.

But now I know, the truth is out,
It's killing me, making me shout,
But now I'm done, hanging from the ceiling,
My face is dead, the rope, no feeling.

So take this as a warning, to stop you too,
From forcing out the truth, from others too,
I hope you don't, for God's sake,
The truth will destroy you, from the day you wake . . .

Andrew Taylor (13)
St Bede's Catholic High School, Lytham

Young Writers Information

We hope you have enjoyed reading this book - and that you will continue to enjoy it in the coming years.

If you like reading and writing poetry drop us a line, or give us a call, and we'll send you a free information pack.

Alternatively if you would like to order further copies of this book or any of our other titles, then please give us a call or log onto our website at www.youngwriters.co.uk

Young Writers Information
Remus House
Coltsfoot Drive
Peterborough
PE2 9JX

(01733) 890066